# GOD'S PRIORITIES

# God's Priorities

J. JOHN

KINGSWAY PUBLICATIONS
EASTBOURNE

ISBN 0 85476 920 X

Published by
KINGSWAY PUBLICATIONS
Lottbridge Drove, Eastbourne, BN23 6NT, England.
Email: books@kingsway.co.uk

Designed and produced for the publishers by
Bookprint Creative Services, P.O. Box 827, BN21 3YJ, England.
Printed in Great Britain.

I dedicate this book to my wife Killy:

'There are many virtuous and capable women in the world, but you surpass them all!' (Proverbs 31:29),

and to my sons Michael, Simeon and Benjamin, who have enriched my life immeasurably and with whom I share the adventure of growing up.

# Contents

# *Acknowledgements*

In writing a book, there are many people who influence the author and make the book a reality.

I am indebted to Chris Walley, a literary surgeon and scholar, who contributed significantly to the process of this book.

To my dear friend Chris Russell (also my researcher). Thank you for your inestimable assistance.

To my good friend and vicar, Mark Stibbe, who provided his considerable expertise in the area of Scripture and theology.

To my colleagues Paul Wilson, Katharine Draper, Charlie Farmery and Amira Kawar – my personal sounding board, and perpetual support group. Thank you, Charlie, for your careful reading of the manuscript. Your suggestions and comments were most helpful.

Thank you to all who so faithfully support me in prayer. Thank you to my trustees, Terry and Juanita Baker, Jamie Colman, Bob Fuller, Mike Shouler and Peter Wright, who encourage and enable me to do this ministry of speaking and writing.

Many thanks to Richard Herkes, Publishing Director of Kingsway: thank you for your faith in me, and thank you for your patience and kindness.

Above all I want to thank the Lord Jesus Christ for his refreshing, steadfast love, and his humorous ability to withstand our capacity to make complex his simple ways!

*J. John*

# *Introduction*

Praying is communicating with God. Through prayer we come to know the all-powerful and loving God, and who he is; through prayer we allow God to direct our lives. I believe that how we pray (or how we do not pray) changes our lives far more than we can ever imagine. Prayer shapes our lives.

The need to pray seems to be built into the heart of all human beings. Even in our allegedly godless Western culture, most people pray at times of crisis to someone or something beyond themselves. It is as if there is an urge to communicate with our Creator so deeply imprinted in the depths of the human mind and heart that it is almost impossible to erase.

Given that prayer is so important and that it is so central to what we are as human beings it was natural for Jesus' followers to ask him to teach them how to pray (Luke 11:1). He answered them by giving the prayer that the church has for centuries called the Lord's Prayer. This is found in Matthew 6:9–10, with a shorter version in Luke 11:2–4, and has been translated into English in various ways. What we might call the Traditional Version, which goes back over 400 years, goes like this:

Our Father, which art in heaven,
hallowed be thy name;
thy kingdom come;
thy will be done,
on earth as it is in heaven.
Give us this day our daily bread.
And forgive us our trespasses,
as we forgive those that trespass against us.
And lead us not into temptation;
but deliver us from evil.
For thine is the kingdom,
the power and the glory,
for ever and ever.
Amen.

A more recent translation, from the New Living Translation, is as follows:

Our Father in heaven,
     may your name be honoured.
May your Kingdom come soon.
May your will be done here on earth,
     just as it is in heaven.
Give us our food for today,
and forgive us our sins,
     just as we have forgiven those who have sinned against us.
And don't let us yield to temptation,
     but deliver us from the evil one.
For yours is the Kingdom and the power and the glory for ever.
Amen.

Most of these changes, which are fairly minor, reflect the way the English language has altered over the intervening centuries.

Before we go any further, think about these two versions of the prayer. In 69 and 78 words respectively, in barely a postcard's worth of text, we have teaching on communicating with God by Jesus. And Jesus was no ordinary man, but claimed, quite uniquely, to be God's Son. That claim was demonstrated by the quality of his life, by his miracles and, above all, by the fact that God raised him from the dead. The fact is that here we have teaching about the most important subject in the world by the man who knew most about it.

In other words, the Lord's Prayer is worth serious study!

## WHO IS THE BOOK FOR?

I have written this book basically for four groups of people.

- Those who have just made a decision to follow Jesus and who want to know how to grow in the Christian life. This is the sort of book that I wish I had been given when I became a Christian 26 years ago.
- Those who have come back to faith after a time away from God.
- Those who know the Lord's Prayer but who feel that they want to get to know and use it better.
- Those who are searching for God and feel that this prayer is a good way to start.

I should say that if you are looking for an academic volume on the origin and history of the Lord's Prayer then you have not found it. There is no part of Jesus' teaching that is more intensely practical than this. We shouldn't be asking ourselves: 'How much do I know about prayer?' but rather, 'How real is prayer to me?' Another question (which we will return frequently to) is: 'How much do my prayers affect my life?'

Be aware then that this is a practical book; it belongs to the same family of things as a manufacturer's instruction manual, a cookbook or even a survival handbook. For those who want to know more about the background of the Lord's Prayer, I have listed some relevant volumes in the Appendix.

One thing that I have particularly tried to do is to address some of the concerns that new Christians might have about this prayer. For example, you might feel happy about using phrases like 'hallowed be your name' and 'your kingdom come' because you grew up with them and they are familiar to you. Alternatively, others might be totally unfamiliar with the prayer. Mind you, being familiar with something and understanding it are two entirely separate things. Even if we have known and used this prayer for many years I think we will find that it does us no harm to look again at the principles of the Lord's Prayer.

I should also say that, in using this book, it doesn't really matter which version of the Lord's Prayer you use. At the start of each section I have given both the Traditional and New Living Translation's version of the phrase being looked at. As we shall see anyway, the point is not the precise words we use but rather that when we pray this prayer (or any other similar prayer) we understand and mean what we are saying.

## WHY PRAY?

In keeping with my claim to try and answer even the most basic questions, let me here try to deal with one that is perhaps the most basic of all: 'Why pray?' After all, someone might say, 'God knows all our needs; why should we waste time troubling him? Can prayer make any difference? Does God really hear me?'

At one level, praying is just something that Christians do and to ask why we do it is to ask an unanswerable question. In part, at least, prayer is a natural communication between our heavenly Father and us. It is – or it should be – as spontaneous as a new baby gurgling to its father or mother. You don't ask why a baby is making chuckling noises as they lie in their mother's arms; they just do it. So there is something that is spontaneous and natural about prayer for a child of God. Our lives without prayer are like lungs without air.

However, prayer does not always come naturally; there are often times when you have to make a choice whether to pray. Sometimes, prayer can be hard work. Sometimes you have other things on your mind, sometimes you feel a million miles away from God. It is at times like these that you have to remind yourself of the reasons for praying. Consider the following four reasons why we should pray.

### 1. Prayer, especially praise in prayer, glorifies God

By praising God we are acknowledging who he is and expressing something of his greatness, goodness and glory. This is vital, for all sorts of reasons.

First, God deserves praise. A desire to praise seems to be built into all human beings. When we are spectators to some achievement, whether it is a sporting feat, a great musical performance or a beautiful painting, it is natural to give praise. We feel that what we have seen or heard deserves praise, whether by a clap of the hands, a letter of appreciation or simply saying 'well done'. That feeling that we ought to praise applies to God. He deserves praise. He is the Creator of all things. We praise Shakespeare's creativity in writing plays; how much more should we praise the one who created Shakespeare? We praise Constable because of his ability to capture in paint the beauty of the English landscape; how much more should we praise the one who made not only Constable but the landscape itself? We praise a singer for a wonderful song; how much more should we praise the one who made music and gave us the ability to hear and appreciate it? Not to praise God would be an act of complete ingratitude.

Second, praising God puts the world into true perspective. Our view of the world, of what we are and of the way things are, is distorted, so we focus on our achievements and problems. People used to believe that the sun circled around the earth. We are prone to a similar spiritual error: that of thinking we are the centre of the universe. And when you have got the basics so badly wrong, as they found with the astronomical error, it is hard to understand anything. Praising God is actually reminding ourselves that God is the centre of the spiritual and moral universe. Only by doing that can we start to make sense of our world.

## 2. Prayer allows us to be involved in God's actions in the world

God doesn't need our prayers; he is perfectly capable of acting on his own initiative. But for some reason he likes to involve us. Like an earthly parent he likes to listen to his children before doing something that might involve them. Think, for example, of the following situation. A father decides that he will build a tree house for his young daughter. He could just get out there with his wood, nails and hammer and make it; after all, he knows better than she does how to build the best sort of tree house. But it is quite likely that a good father will sit down with his daughter and ask whether she wants a tree house, what tree she would like it in and what shape she thinks would look best. Oh, and what colour would she like it? I'm sure you can imagine the conversation. What is the father doing here? The reality is that he doesn't need to ask his daughter anything – he knows it all already. The fact of the matter is that, in his love for his daughter, the father wants to involve her in the decision-making so that she feels that the tree house is something she has worked on. In prayer God chooses to involve us.

## 3. Prayer allows us to enjoy fellowship with God by communicating with him

This is very important. Christianity is ultimately about the relationship between God and us, and in order for a relationship to form and to be maintained there has to be communication. Prayer is the communication that keeps a Christian's relationship with God fresh, healthy and real.

We need to remember that prayer is not just us talking to God – that would be a very strange way of maintaining a relationship – but also God being able to talk to us. Prayer should never be considered as a one-way phone call like a message left on an answering machine. It allows us to hear God speak back and it is vital that we listen. If we would have God hear us when we pray, we must hear him when he speaks. How does God speak? In my experience, God most commonly speaks to me through an inaudible but unmistakable prompting of my mind and heart, but at other times he can speak in more dramatic ways. Other people's experience varies. The important thing is that prayer is a dialogue and through it we grow spiritually. Just as the communication between two people in a relationship can have a large element that is not spoken (for example, through body language), then there is in the same way more that goes on in prayer than just an exchange of words.

## 4. Prayer allows us to receive God's priorities for our lives

This too is very important. We live in a world that is hostile to God and all that he stands for. Every day, Christians are getting an almost constant stream of persuasive messages, either open or subtly disguised, to try to make our priorities those of the rest of the world. Advertising, TV, our workplace, all say things like: 'Look after yourself first', 'Cheat but don't get caught', 'It's fun to play around sexually' and so on. Prayer (along with reading God's word, the Bible) allows us to adjust our values to those of God. Many companies regularly tune in to the radio to get the exact time signal so that they can reset all their equipment to an exact and standard time. Prayer performs a similar function: it allows us to set our lives to God's exact and perfect way of living.

## THE LAYOUT OF THE BOOK

Before looking at the Lord's Prayer itself, we will consider briefly what Jesus says about praying in the verses in Matthew's Gospel that come just before the prayer. I cover this in the short chapter called 'The Preliminaries of Prayer'. The main part of this book is then devoted to going through the Lord's Prayer phrase by phrase.

Before we go further, let me discuss something that may seem to be of very little value but is in fact very significant. It centres on the question: 'Did Jesus pray this prayer himself?' Some people point out that as he was without sin himself, Jesus could not have prayed, 'Forgive us our sins.' I understand their concern and if the prayer were worded 'forgive *me my* sins' I would agree, but the prayer here, as elsewhere, is plural and communal; it asks that God would 'forgive *us our* sins'. I think it is perfectly possible that as Jesus so closely identified with sinful humanity, he might well have prayed this prayer on behalf of his people. If you think Jesus did not pray this prayer, then there is the danger that you think of the Lord's Prayer as a pattern that he gave but did not follow himself.

It is more helpful to think of this as being a prayer that is modelled, as closely as possible, on Jesus' own prayer life. The Lord's Prayer was a response to the disciples seeing Jesus praying and saying, 'Show us how you did it.' If you think this is close to what Jesus himself prayed, then the prayer acquires a new significance. If you accept that prayer shapes our lives and we become what we pray, then adopting Jesus' own prayer helps us to become like him. By giving his disciples this prayer Jesus is giving them and us a way of imitating him. Imagine being trained by an expert in some difficult procedure, like playing a complex piano piece or assembling a piece of furniture. The expert might say, 'Watch me, see where I put my hands, copy me.' The idea would be that, by imitation, you would become like the expert. I believe that this is what Jesus wants us to do with the Lord's Prayer. In fact, if we want to imitate Christ and grow to become more like him, I can think of no better way than by using this prayer as a pattern for our own praying.

Jesus gave the Lord's Prayer to his followers as a pattern for them to follow and therefore it is not surprising that there is a clear structure within it. In fact the Lord's Prayer is like a letter: there is an opening address ('Dear X or Y'), a series of brief requests or petitions ('Please do this or that') and then a final signing off. The prayer includes five requests; the first two focus on what God desires and the last three on what we need.

We can summarise the structure of the Lord's Prayer as follows and I have used a single word beginning with P to give the theme of each unit.

## Opening

- The prayer begins with an address that states who it is we pray to and what our relationship is with them. In doing this it reminds us of the *privilege* of prayer.

## Praying for what God desires

- We *praise* all that God is and does.
- We acknowledge that God's *purpose* for us and our world comes above everything else.

## Praying for what we need

- We pray for our *provision*, asking God for those things that we need for our physical life.
- We pray for our *pardon*, asking God for forgiveness and that we in turn forgive others.
- We pray for our *protection* from the devil and from being defeated by life's trials.

## Conclusion

- The Lord's Prayer ends with a sentence that reminds us of what our *perspective* on life should be.

These seven themes – privilege, praise, purpose, provision, pardon, protection and perspective – form the headings of the chapters that make up the main part of this book. At the end of each chapter I have given some questions designed to help you reflect further.

# 1

# The Preliminaries of Prayer

*And now about prayer. When you pray, don't be like the hypo-crites who love to pray publicly on street corners and in the syn-agogues where everyone can see them. I assure you, that is all the reward they will ever get. But when you pray, go away by your-self, shut the door behind you, and pray to your Father secretly. Then your Father, who knows all secrets, will reward you.*

*When you pray, don't babble on and on as people of other relig-ions do. They think their prayers are answered only by repeating their words again and again. Don't be like them, because your Father knows exactly what you need even before you ask him!*

*Pray like this . . .*

(Matthew 6:5–9)

## THREE PRINCIPLES

The Lord's Prayer occurs in Matthew's Gospel as part of a long section of teaching (Matthew 5:1–7:27) that has become known as the Sermon on the Mount because of the reference (in Matthew 5:1) that it was given by Jesus to his disciples on a hill. In chapter 6 Jesus talks about three traditional religious activities: giving to the poor, praying and fasting. For each activity he points out how it can be done wrongly and how his disciples ought to do it differently.

With prayer, Jesus points out two examples of how not to do it. One example of a wrong way to pray is to treat prayer as an opportunity to show off to others. It was apparently the practice in Jesus' day for people to pray where everyone could see them. As a result, you could get a wonderful reputation for being holy. Jesus calls such people hypocrites or play-actors; they pretend to be glorifying God, but in reality they are just trying to impress others so that they glorify themselves. Their prayer is a sham. The danger that Jesus warns of here has not gone away. When we are praying with others it is all too easy to come up with some fine phrases or impressive words. But we must always ask ourselves whether our public praying has some element of trying to impress people. While other people may be impressed, God is not!

There are other dangers. For instance, we can all too easily give the impression that we pray more, or better, than we actually do. We may say to someone going through a tough patch, 'I'll pray for you.' But are we saying that for their comfort or our reputation?

The other example of a wrong way of praying that Jesus mentions is mechanically and mindlessly repeating words as if that would improve the effectiveness of the prayer. This, Jesus says, is nonsense; as an all-seeing heavenly Father, God knows the needs of his children. Jesus is not saying here that long prayers are wrong; he prayed all night on some occasions (Luke 6:12). There is a world of difference between spending a long time praying and using lots of words without thinking about them. Nor is Jesus saying that repetition in prayer is wrong; he repeated his words in the Garden of Gethsemane (Mark 14:39). What he is criticising here is a robotic piling up of empty phrases, because behind them lies a wrong idea of God. What Jesus is saying is that we must never use prayer as a way of manipulating God, because God is above being manipulated by us. If we ever think we can manipulate God then we have got totally the wrong idea about our relationship with him.

Jesus uses these two examples of the wrong way of praying to make the point about what real prayer is. There are three principles in this passage that, as we come to the Lord's Prayer, we will need to remember.

## Principle 1: Real prayer involves a *personal* relationship

First, real prayer is something that is personal and intimate: 'But when you pray, go away by yourself, shut the door behind you, and pray to your Father secretly.' Privacy would have been hard when, like Jesus' original hearers, you lived with a large family in a single-roomed house. Probably the only place with any privacy would have been the storeroom in which valuables were kept. And what Jesus is saying is, 'Go to the storeroom, close the door behind you and there pray alone.' The point he is making is that prayer is something between God and you alone. It is a private matter and in our conversation with God it is best if there is just the two of us. Of course there is public prayer, but it is something totally different and is never a replacement for private prayer. It has been said that the secret of prayer is prayer in secret. As a word of advice, if you pray publicly better than you pray privately be careful; you may be in danger of acting a part. Remember too that whether you pray on your own or publicly the only really important member of the audience is God. However, the Lord's Prayer also gives a balancing truth: we pray alone but we also pray as part of the family of God. This is something we will return to.

---

**The secret of prayer is prayer in secret.**

---

Jesus suggests that our praying is a personal conversation with God. Actually some people find it helps their concentration if they say their prayers aloud rather than just thinking them in their heads. And if you do that, then privacy is essential.

Incidentally, don't get confused; there is a common belief, especially in Britain, that it is not just prayer that is a private matter but *all* religion. The result is that many people grow up never talking about what they believe and many Christians never talk about Jesus with others. They have got it all wrong; our prayer life ought to be between God and us while everything else is a public matter. In fact, as we shall see, if we have truly met with God in prayer then our public life will certainly reflect that fact.

## Principle 2: Real prayer involves a *living* relationship

Behind all that Jesus says here (and in fact the whole Bible) is the truth that God is a living being. This is an important fact that is all too easily overlooked. Praying is not us expressing our inner concerns to the empty air; it is us talking to a God who lives, knows, hears and acts. Wow! That's why making a public ceremony out of our praying is nonsense. It insults God and it misuses the privilege of being able to talk to him. Owing to the fact that God is alive, real prayer ought to be intelligent and meaningful.

Imagine if someone came to see you, sat down in front of you and then babbled out nothing more than a tremendously long string of words about how wonderful you were and what a privilege it was to meet you. After a while, you would feel irritated by the fact that your visitor wasn't really talking to you. If they returned the next day and repeated further strings of empty words then I imagine that you would definitely feel insulted. I could see God feeling the same about mechanical prayers. We are not to treat him as an inanimate object or force. He is a personal God; we can talk and communicate with him and we can offer him real praises and real petitions.

Let me mention at this point something that will come up again later but which arises naturally out of Jesus' teaching here. Because we have a living relationship with God, we need to use living language with him. I say this because Christians can get the idea from hearing other people pray publicly that the only way God can be addressed is with really formal and old-fashioned words. Phrases such as 'we beseech thee' are very misleading to those who do not understand them. Some things are only ever delicately hinted at, so that people do not die but rather 'go to be with the Lord'. This odd form of English ('Special Prayer English') is also spoken in a strangely reverent way that is quite unlike the normal tone of the speaker.

Don't get me wrong. I am not mocking either these words, the real feelings they doubtless express or those who use them. But I do want to point out the real problems associated with using this sort of language.

- It can be a barrier to new Christians. If they feel that they must master this strange religious form of English in order to be able to pray publicly, some may feel, for example, that they need to address God as 'thee' privately.

- It gives a very old-fashioned feel to public prayer. In some churches you can get the impression that you have walked into a radio set for a Victorian historical drama. Of course reverence for God is very right and proper, but does reverence have to involve ancient English? No! Actually, using this sort of Special Prayer English can sometimes disguise the fact that we are not really thinking about what we are saying.

- Perhaps the biggest problem with Special Prayer English lies in another area. It disguises the fact that prayer is based on a real and living relationship with God. If you use plain modern twenty-first-century English in everyday speech, then why not use it in prayer? By using an artificial language to talk with God we have somehow started to separate prayer from the 'real world'. The danger of separating our faith from our day-to-day lives is something that will come up again as we look through the Lord's Prayer.

Prayer is all about a living relationship with God. Let's never forget it.

## Principle 3: Prayer involves a *family* relationship

The term Jesus uses here to describe God to his disciples is 'Father' and that idea underlies all that the Lord's Prayer is about. I will talk more about the term 'Father' in the next chapter, but the point here is that it alters the whole basis of prayer. Prayer, for the Christian, is talking and listening to our loving and caring heavenly Father. Prayer is not about performing a routine to persuade, or calm down, a harsh distant God; it is having a trusting relationship with the God who cares for us. Those who have come to faith in Jesus from other religions generally say that this new relationship is the most wonderful thing about their newfound faith. They have gone from knowing God only as a servant might know some distant unpredictable and often harsh master, to knowing him as a son or a daughter knows a loving parent. The title one convert from Islam gave her autobiography says it all: *I Dared to Call Him Father* (Bilquis Sheikh: Kingsway Publications, 1979).

Actually, behind the idea of us praying to God as our heavenly Father lies more than just a family relationship; it is the idea of being dependent. I'm sure you have heard the expression 'dependants' in the context of the family; for example you read of 'a working mum and three dependants – two children and her father'. The three *depend* upon her supplying their needs. A child is totally dependent – every need must be supplied by their parents. In the same way a Christian is dependent on God. We have nothing we can offer God to make him accept us; we must simply accept God's forgiving kindness or grace towards us. Some people, at times all of us, find this hard to take. It seems just too much that God should do it all. We want to contribute. But the fact is that this is the only relationship we can have with him. We are sinners, we stand under judgement, and all we can do is ask for his forgiveness and humbly accept it when it is given. We are dependants.

When you or I come and pray to God, what happens is that there is a meeting between him and us. If I were to ask people to imagine that meeting in picture terms, I would expect that many would describe it in terms of some powerless peasant grovelling on the red-carpeted floor of some vast hall before the foot of an awesome throne on which solemnly sits an even more awe-inspiring king. That, to them, would be what prayer is about. Yet the language of the New Testament is that when followers of Jesus pray, the meeting between them and God is much more like a family meeting. The New Testament does not downplay the majesty of God; he still has a throne (read the book of Revelation), but it points out that to be a Christian is to have an enormous privilege. Whereas once we could only ever meet with God as King or Judge, if we have become followers of Jesus, we can now meet with God as a heavenly Father. It is as if, when he meets us now, the king takes his robes and crown off, ushers us into a side room and there says, 'My child, let's talk.' The relationship between God and Jesus' followers is that of a father and his children.

These three principles, that real prayer involves a personal, living and family relationship with God, raise a question that must be dealt with before any of us can go any further. It is whether we are in God's family.

## THE NEED TO BE IN GOD'S FAMILY

The Bible teaches that when a believer in Christ comes before God, he or she comes to him as a child before their father, not as a citizen before their king. We are graciously adopted as members of God's family. I wish that all I had to do here was to reassure you, whoever and wherever you are, that you really are a member of God's family and encourage you to go ahead and pray this family prayer.

However, I can give no such reassurance. You see you cannot properly pray this prayer (or any other prayer that calls God 'Father' and relies on the father–child relationship) unless you actually are a member of God's family. All logic goes against it. Imagine going up to someone and saying with trust in your voice, 'Father – Dad – I need some help.' The only person you could do that to would be someone who really was your father. Otherwise it is a nonsensical and even offensive request that is likely to get the obvious response 'Clear off! You are no child of mine!' In fact the early church used to prohibit people from saying the Lord's Prayer until they were baptised in Christ. The reasoning was the same. Only God's children can have the privilege of calling God 'Father'.

This is of vital importance. The Lord's Prayer assumes that we have become part of God's family. This is why it has been suggested that the prayer be called 'the Disciple's Prayer'. Many people pray this prayer but tragically are not actually in God's family and as a result are presuming on a relationship that does not exist. Because this is such an important point and because it is so often misunderstood I want to spend some time talking about how we become a child of God.

It is common today to think of God as being the heavenly Father of everybody. According to the Bible there actually is a sense in which God is the Father of all human beings (see, for example, Acts 17:28), but this seems to go no further than that God has made or created everybody. The Bible however is clear that we are not all, in the fullest sense of the expression, 'God's children'. To be able to address God as 'Father' with any confidence you need to be in the right relationship with him. Simply being human does not automatically qualify you to be a son or daughter of God. But it does mean that the opportunity to be part of God's family is open to you.

The Bible is plain that to be in that right relationship with God, to be a true child of God, is something that can only be obtained through Jesus. Being a child of God is a privilege that Jesus extends to those who are his followers.

So how do we get to be in God's family and have the right to call God 'Father'? And why is Jesus so important? The Bible uses many images to describe the way Jesus has made it possible for us to become accepted by God, but here I want to concentrate on this area of relationships. Let me list five key points.

First, human beings were created to be in a right relationship with God. We were designed to be his children in the richest meaning of the word. The first chapter of the book of Genesis talks about men and women being made in God's image and part of what that means is that we were given the ability to freely relate to God and to communicate with him. In the images of paradise used in the first few chapters of Genesis the picture is given of a free, unhindered and perfect relationship between God and humanity. Indeed, Luke 3:38 talks about Adam being the son of God; God had made him, and he and Eve must have known God as their Father.

Second, the relationship between humanity and God has been broken. In Genesis 3 we read how the first human couple, Adam and Eve, rebelled against God by disobeying him and then, under God's judgement, were exiled from Eden. The relationship was broken. Adam and Eve chose to be separated from God and ever since then, the human race has lived in a similar manner as rebels against God. One of Jesus' most famous stories, the story of the Lost Son (Luke 15:11–31), tells of a young man who rebelled against his father, turned his back on him and went off to a distant land, where his life soon descended into total misery. This tale of a broken relationship with a father, a departure from the family home and a miserable fate in a self-imposed exile, is a replay of the Adam and Eve story. It is also our story and the story of every human being, except one, who has ever lived. Other than Jesus, everyone has turned their back on God and lost the privileges of being a child of God. Twice in the story of the Lost Son we hear the young man admit that he has sinned against his father and is no longer worthy of being called his son. That is where the human race has ended up: spiritually separated and hungry and having thrown away any right to be a child of God.

Third, no human action can restore that lost relationship. Our offences against God's love and kindness to us are so serious that we cannot restore the breach that has been made. In the story of the Lost Son, by asking his father for his inheritance the young man had effectively wished him dead. In the culture of his time he had committed an outrageous and unpardonable offence against his father by his rebellious actions. We have done the same by our attitudes and actions. We read that as he was dying of hunger, the young man in Jesus' story came to his senses and decided to set off home to confess his sin against his father in the hope that he might be taken back as a hired servant. He knew that he had lost all hope of going back to being a son; he dared to hope that he might be taken on as a servant. That idea of being accepted as a servant rather than as a child represents the best hope that, on our own, we could ever have of being accepted by God. Even by saying sorry and admitting the wrongness of our actions to God, all that we could reasonably expect is that God might allow us to enter into a new relationship with him, but only as a servant. This actually represents the best hope that any religion based on human efforts could offer: the hope that God might accept us as servants.

Fourth, God has amazingly intervened, at enormous cost, to restore the relationship between himself and humanity. While all that we could reasonably expect is to be treated as servants, God's love and compassion go wonderfully beyond that. The great story of the Bible is that out of love, God became involved in the human race in order to provide the way for us to be brought back to him. Throughout the story of the Old Testament we see God making a special nation and teaching them about himself and his holiness. To this special people God promised that he would one day send someone who would restore the broken relationship and would bring men and women back to him. Finally, in the person of Jesus Christ, God himself became one of us. Jesus' life was marked by complete obedience to God and a perfect relationship with God as his Father. In everything Jesus did and said, he showed the pattern of what we were meant to be as God's sons and daughters. Yet Jesus was more than the perfect example of what it means to be a child of God. He chose a course of action that meant he would inevitably be crucified. There are many ways of under-standing what that horrible death meant and what it achieved. Thinking as we are here in terms of relationships, I want to point out that it is no accident that the crucifixion was the punishment for rebels and revolutionaries. In the gospels we read that Jesus was crucified between two 'criminals', but the Greek word used may here mean 'rebels' or 'guerrillas'. What an irony! The one who had never rebelled against God was executed for rebellion! Yet in a way that is the whole point. He took the punishment for rebellion that we would otherwise pay. He took our place. The apostle Paul expresses this wonderful exchange clearly: 'So I live my life in this earthly body by trusting in the Son of God, who loved me and gave himself for me' (Galatians 2:20). To understand this awesome exchange is fundamental to becoming a child of God and knowing God as a Father. In the story of the Lost Son, we read of the father's love. As the son returned, while he was still a long way away, his father saw him (how long had he been watching?) and ran out to greet him; and filled with love and compassion, embraced and kissed him. The father then welcomed the lost son back, not as a servant, but as a son. The father's forgiving love reached out to his lost son.

Fifth, through Jesus, God has completely and wonderfully restored the broken relationship. The penalty of our rebellion has been paid through Jesus' death. In the parable of the Lost Son we read how the father said, 'Quick! Bring the finest robe in the house and put it on him. Get a ring for his finger, and sandals for his feet. And kill the calf we have been fattening in the pen. We must celebrate with a feast, for this son of mine was dead and has now returned to life. He was lost, but now he is found.' The one who was a rebel is now declared to be a son and given the symbols of sonship; the one who was effectively dead is now pronounced alive. The young man is restored back to the position he once had, of being a dearly loved son. This is a wonderful picture of what it is to be made right with God through Jesus. Proof that our relationship to God has been restored through Jesus is given in two ways. One is by the resurrection; the other is the giving of the Holy Spirit. The first is a fact of public history, the other a matter of our personal experience. In the book of Romans, while discussing how Christians are to deal with sinful desires, the apostle Paul says:

> For all who are led by the Spirit of God are children of God. So you should not be like cowering, fearful slaves. You should behave instead like God's very own children, adopted into his family – calling him 'Father, dear Father.' For his Holy Spirit speaks to us deep in our hearts and tells us that we are God's children. And since we are his children, we will share his treasures – for everything God gives to his Son, Christ, is ours, too. (Romans 8:14–17)

Do you see the pattern here? If we have received the Holy Spirit, the gift God gives to all who have become believers in Christ, we are no longer slaves but are now God's 'very own children' and are adopted into his family. A great summary of this whole process of conversion is given at the start of John's Gospel where John, writing of Jesus, says, 'But to all who believed him and accepted him, he gave the right to become children of God' (John 1:12). Paul in Galatians 3:26 says something very similar: 'So you are all children of God through faith in Christ Jesus.'

Let me now make two comments about these five points. First of all, to become a Christian is to have more than a head understanding of these facts. It requires a personal decision. God has made a way for us to go back to him; Jesus has paid the price of our rebellion. Yet, like the lost son, we must get up and go towards him, admitting our sin and our need for forgiveness. Linked with this is the necessity for us to be able to accept this great offer and trust in it for ourselves. The basis of a personal faith in Christ is not 'Jesus died for mankind', but the spine-tingling, hair-raising, shiver-down-the-spine fact that 'he died for *me*'. It is not enough to have been born into a Christian family or even to be a churchgoer. Church membership doesn't make you a Christian any more than owning a piano makes you a pianist. It is vital that you personally know you are a child of God.

Second, these five points have been given in an orderly and logical sequence:

1.  God loves us and wants a relationship with us.
2.  We have rebelled against God, breaking that relationship.
3.  We cannot restore that relationship ourselves.
4.  Through Christ, God has made a costly intervention to bring us back to himself.
5.  Through faith in Christ we can enjoy a restored relationship with God.

Now this step-by-step arrangement – or something very like it – is a very useful way of ordering in our minds what it means to become a Christian. It is a good summary of what the gospel (the good news of Jesus) is all about and I have covered these statements in more detail in my book *Calling Out* (Word, 2000). The thing is that while some people become Christians by understanding these steps in a nice neat 1, 2, 3, 4, 5 order, not everybody does. I say this because some people get worried about whether or not they are Christians because they themselves did not go through this sequence of steps. Perhaps, for example, they made a decision to follow Jesus and only afterwards came to realise that they had been in rebellion against God.

Actually I suspect that the logical steps idea is misleading. After all, we are talking relationships here, and they are far from logical! I think that most of us start off the Christian life with a rather sketchy grasp of what is what and over time God fills in our understanding more and more. In fact many of the contacts Jesus had with people in the Gospels, or those recounted in the Acts of the Apostles, show that there wasn't a rigid pattern of them coming to him. In fact there are cases where people seem to meet Christ, be accepted by him and only then do the implications of that sink in. Think, for example, of Zacchaeus (Luke 19:1–10). Perhaps it is best to think of these points not as logical steps but as the five rootlets of some plant that, if it is to grow, must all eventually be put down. The advantage of such an image is that it suggests that our knowledge can, and should, be deepened over time.

So don't be put off if you did not become a Christian by working through these points one by one, but came to Christ by another and possibly longer road. The key point is that now you have acknowledged your rebellion against God, have trusted in Christ for forgiveness and know something of the presence, peace and power of the Holy Spirit. If you understand this, you have come back from exile as a rebel and are accepted as a son or daughter of God. You can now pray to your Father God using the prayer Jesus has given. It was written for you and you are fully entitled to use it.

## So how do we use the Lord's Prayer?

Finally, before we look at the Lord's Prayer itself I think it is important to consider how we use it. In some traditions the habit has been to repeat the exact wording of the Lord's Prayer either in private praying or in the course of a church service. Although I do both, I think there are dangers in *only* using the prayer like this. In fact I am firmly convinced that rather than being something to be precisely copied, this prayer is really a template for our praying. It is a framework not a formula; a pattern prayer not a parrot prayer.

---

**It is a pattern prayer not a parrot prayer.**

---

I have four reasons for saying this:

- In Matthew 6:9 Jesus says that we are to pray *like* this, not *pray this*.
- Although the version of the Lord's Prayer in Luke 11:1–4 has the same outline as Matthew's version, its wording is different. This suggests there never was only one fixed version.
- As we have seen, Jesus has just been critical of prayers that are empty rituals. It would be strange if immediately after saying this he had given a formula prayer.
- Taken to its logical conclusion this belief could mean that we should pray the prayer in Aramaic, the language that Jesus would have used when he gave it to his disciples.

So while we may use the Lord's Prayer as part of a service or public worship, I think the best use of it in our personal praying is to think of the sections as sub-divisions or headings. When we pray we can fill in the details of each section as appropriate. So when we come to the section I have called 'Provision' we could pray, 'Give us our food for today' and then spend some time specifically asking God for those things we physically need before moving on to 'Pardon' ('Forgive us our sins . . .').

The one thing we ought never to do in prayer is get ourselves in a groove where we end up praying the same way, day in and day out. To reach the point where a meeting with God is dull and boring is to go against everything Jesus teaches about prayer here and elsewhere. In using the Lord's Prayer as a pattern we need to keep it alive.


## QUESTIONS

- The point has been made that prayer is like a letter or a conversation (by phone or email, if not face to face). What are the good points and the weak points about such a comparison?
- In some church traditions the Lord's Prayer is said or sung every week. Is this a good idea? What safeguards should be introduced? How do we avoid getting into a routine with praying?
- How can we remind ourselves that what we are doing in prayer is enjoying a relationship and not enacting a ritual?

# 2
# Privilege

*Our Father, which art in heaven,*
(Traditional)

*Our Father in heaven,*
(New Living Translation)

## INTRODUCTION

A NASA official at the Kennedy Space Centre was explaining to a reporter the complexities of sending human beings to Mars. The reporter asked about how the crew would return to Earth. 'That involves a highly complex plan,' the representative said, 'and it begins with the words "Our Father, which art in heaven".'

These six words have become a shorthand for prayer. But what do they mean? How often do we even think about what they mean? In this chapter I want to unpack what they ought to mean to us.

How you address a letter is important; do you put 'Dear Jim', 'Dear Sir' or 'Dear Mr Smith'? It's not just etiquette; it reflects how you relate to that person. The tone of a letter starting 'My Dear Jane' will be very different from one that starts

'Dear Madam'. Prayer works in a similar way. No prayer would be complete without some sort of opening address; it expresses who it is we are praying to. In fact, so necessary is some sort of address to our prayers that the story is told of the man who was so thoroughly confused in his beliefs that when he felt he had to pray, the only words he could think of to start it with were 'To whom it may concern'.

This opening phrase, 'Our Father in heaven', sets the framework in which we pray and when we look at it, we realise that when the Christian prays, he or she enters into an extraordinary privilege.

There are three vital things to learn from this first phrase about our privilege. We have a child's privilege, we have an awesome privilege and we have a shared privilege.

## A child's privilege: a *Father* in heaven

In the Aramaic in which the Lord's Prayer was first spoken and in the Greek language in which the gospels were written down, the first word of the prayer is 'Father'. In fact Luke's version omits the 'our' entirely and starts simply with 'Father'.

Using the word 'father' as a way of addressing God is something that seems to have been characteristic of Jesus and which may well have been unique to him. He made a habit of using the Aramaic word *Abba* when he prayed to God (Mark 14:36), and *Abba* was a word that a child would call his or her father. We might translate it as something like 'Daddy' or 'Dad'; it is loving and trusting as well as respectful. The fact that Jesus regularly and consistently used the term *Abba* of God was something that was so distinctive and precious that over 20 years after his crucifixion

and resurrection Christians who spoke no Aramaic were reg
using the word (Romans 8:15–16; Galatians 4:6–7).

The truth that followers of Jesus are children of God is one
of the great notes of joy that echo throughout the New
Testament. For example, to return to the passage from Romans
8 we looked at in the last chapter, we read:

> For all who are led by the Spirit of God are children of God. So you
> should not be like cowering, fearful slaves. You should behave
> instead like God's very own children, adopted into his family –
> calling him "Father, dear Father." For his Holy Spirit speaks to us
> deep in our hearts and tells us that we are God's children. And since
> we are his children, we will share his treasures – for everything God
> gives to his Son, Christ, is ours, too. But if we are to share his glory,
> we must also share his suffering. (Romans 8:14–17)

There are many other verses about us being brought into
God's family and I have found my friend Mark Stibbe's book,
*From Orphans to Heirs*, very helpful here. In fact all the lan-
guage of 'Dear Brothers and Sisters' that we find in the New
Testament letters was not fancy over-the-top words; it was
reality. Whether they were a Jew or a non-Jew, a slave or slave-
owner, a beggar or philosopher, if they became followers of
Jesus they were one, they were *family*.

This idea that God is a loving heavenly Father who listens to
us is a wonderful concept that should form the basis of all our
praying. As Christians we can come to God with the intimacy
that Jesus did, because as Christians we are united to Jesus
through the Holy Spirit. As such we now have, through Christ,
the extraordinary privilege of being able to come to God on

the same basis as he did. True, we are sinful and he was not and we do not have the knowledge of God that he had, but if God has indeed adopted us into his family, then we too are children. We can know God as Father.

I realise that the word 'father' is a difficult one these days. I am all too aware that there are people who have suffered at the hands of their fathers and, for such people, referring to God as 'Father' raises only bad associations. But the concept that God is the Christian's heavenly Father is so vital that to let such an experience deprive you of the knowledge of God as Father is to let your past seriously rob you. It is hard here to offer any simple advice that will not sound trite, but I make three cautious suggestions.

• It may help to keep reminding yourself that what you endured came not from a father as God intended fathers to be but from a poor imitation. God is the authentic, perfect Father whose love is pure and whose desires towards you are solely for your good. It is God who defines what the image of 'father' should mean, not humans. All fathers (and I speak as a father of three sons) fail, but some fail so badly as to cease to be fathers in anything other than a biological sense.

• It is the concept of the word 'father' that is important, not the word itself. If the word 'father' has unhappy associations for you, then you may want to use an alternative word. You could, for instance, use *Abba*. The important thing though is for you to define your alternative using the images and language the Bible uses about God. In this way you let God's reality rather than your past experience mould the image of fatherhood.

- You may find that it helps to talk things through with a trained and sympathetic counsellor.

Let me return to the positives. If we are members of God's family then when we come to God we are entitled to address him as 'Father'. It is a tremendous privilege to know God as Father. Many people, including some who pray this prayer, do not know God except as a far-off, grim and often terrifying Ruler. For them prayer is like a medieval peasant trying to gain an audience with the king. The best they can expect is a few brief minutes of royal attention and it is far more likely that they will be imprisoned or executed for their impertinence to try.

The good news of Jesus Christ is that we who come to God through him are no longer servants. We are now sons and daughters and we have the privilege to come before God knowing with confidence that he loves and hears us. One of Jesus' disciples, the apostle John, wrote, 'See how very much our heavenly Father loves us, for he allows us to be called his children, and we really are!' (1 John 3:1).

## An awesome privilege: a Father *in heaven*

One of the wonderful things about the Lord's Prayer is the balance held within it. This first phrase displays this very well. God is our Father but he is also a Father *in heaven*. What does this mean?

Of course the word 'heaven' is a problem for many people. There is a common view that heaven is a place somewhere 'up there', probably several billion light years away, where angels dressed in white nightdresses play harps on fluffy clouds and from where God peers down on us. The reality is in fact somewhat different.

Let me make three points about heaven that are relevant here.

## 1. Heaven is an awesome reality

First, it may be helpful to think of heaven being located not in some unbelievably distant place, but in another dimension. Although invisible to us, heaven is not far from us. That means that praying to God does not represent the ultimate in long-distance phone calls. Second, heaven is not insubstantial. To use another illustration, it may help you to think of all that we see around us, our home, our town, our world, as nothing more than an enormous theatre set. Offstage, invisible to us as we are absorbed in the ongoing drama of our lives, lies heaven with God and the angels. And although our little play seems like reality to us, in comparison to heaven it is little more than a canvas and plaster stage set. And one day as we read through our script we will realise that our part has come to an end and we will walk off and face the reality of heaven, whether we want to or not. In fact one day, perhaps sooner rather than later, there will be a great shout from offstage, the lights will come on and the whole play will be ended.

Heaven, and the God who dwells in heaven, are the solid and holy realities that lie all around us. When you pray, remind yourself of this; you are connecting to the real world.

## 2. Heaven is a place of awesome power and majesty

The psalmist wrote: 'I lift my eyes to you, O God, enthroned in heaven' (Psalm 123:1). Heaven, this real place just out of sight but never far from us, is also the place of God's throne. This suggests that when we think of heaven we need to always think of the majesty and glory that belong to God. We always need to remember this aspect of who God is.

The Old Testament is very helpful, particularly in passages such as Genesis 1–2:4, in some of the Psalms (e.g. Psalms 66, 76, 93, 97) and passages in Isaiah (e.g. 40:10–31). God dwells in the centre of power of the universe. Think of this world's places of power – Whitehall, Washington, the Kremlin and so on – and multiply them infinitely. Heaven is that. From heaven the entire universe, from the smallest amoeba to the most distant galaxy, is run.

There is an enormous indescribable greatness and glory to God that we mustn't forget. It is, or should be, a humbling thought that in prayer we are dealing with a God whose power is such that he only had to speak and the universe was created. We meet with a God who is eternal, all-seeing, all-knowing and all-controlling; a God who has both the delicacy to construct a butterfly and the strength to control exploding galaxies. That is what heaven is about and we are fools if we forget it. That is why praise is so essential; it is expressing our appreciation of the fact that God is so great and wonderful. The only right response to the majesty that is God is praise and adoration.

---

**God doesn't just desire to do us good, he is infinitely able to.**

---

This is also, or should be, an encouraging thought. In prayer we meet with the one who has the power to help us. For someone to aid another person means they have to be both willing to help and able to help. If we are willing to help someone but do not have the resources to help them, then we are powerless. All we can do is wring our hands in frustration and say something feeble like, 'I really sympathise. I feel your pain. I'm right behind you.' The great first phrase of the Lord's Prayer reminds us that God is both willing and able. 'Our Father' is a reminder that God is willing to help us and that he desires to do us good. However, the 'in heaven' clause reminds us that he has unlimited resources available. God doesn't just desire to do us good, he is infinitely able to. When we come to God we should realise he is not powerless but rather that he is great and mighty. In tough times that can be a real comfort.

I must reluctantly add a caution here. Yes, God is willing and God is able, but that doesn't mean he will automatically answer our prayers in the way we want him to. Most of us would be in trouble if all our prayers had been answered. God knows what is best for us and just as a father does not give a child everything that he or she asks for, so God doesn't always just sign 'Approved' at the end of our prayers. To use modern legal language, we could say that God 'reserves the right to answer prayer requests in such a way as to be in our best long-term interest'. Anyone who has been a Christian for any length of time can think of prayers they made about which they can now say, with a shudder of relief, 'Thank you, Father, for not answering that one!'

Jesus himself, who set the perfect pattern for how we should pray, knew the Father's right to overrule our prayers. When, on the night before his crucifixion, Jesus prayed in the Garden of Gethsemane, Matthew 26:39 records what happened: 'He went on a little farther and fell face down on the ground, praying, "My Father! If it is possible, let this cup of suffering be taken away from me. Yet I want your will, not mine."' 'Your will, not mine' is the key phrase to add on to the end of our prayers.

I acknowledge though that there are situations when phrases like this seem trite and almost insulting, for example when someone we love is suffering or when evil seems to be running wild in our lives. Then, quite frankly, we feel that it is just not fair that God doesn't act. There are no easy intellectual and logical answers. I can only offer two thoughts here. The first is that we need to be open and honest with God at such times and to feel able to express our feelings. There is a danger in pretending that we are really all right when we are not. The Bible includes many examples of people such as Job, David and Jesus who were real with God in prayer and who were able to tell him how they felt. Second, sometimes the darkness is so deep that all we can do is trust in God and keep going. The Bible suggests that on the cross, Jesus himself knew something of this darkness as he suffered for us. The cry of 'My God, my God, why have you forsaken me?' (Matthew 27:46; Mark 15:34) is more than a quotation of the first verse of Psalm 22; it reflects a genuine sense of loss and desolation. The reality is that there is no road so dark that Christ has not travelled it before – although for some going through difficult times this may seem to give little comfort!

But let us return to answered prayer. And here, when we pray to our Father in heaven about things, we need to remember that we pray to the one whose power is so enormous that we cannot comprehend its vastness. The apostle Paul was evidently seized with a similar thought when he wrote in Ephesians:

'Now glory be to God! By his mighty power at work within us, he is able to accomplish infinitely more than we would ever dare to ask or hope' (Ephesians 3:20).

Because prayer connects us to heaven it has a serious potential. But do you and I really enter into everything that is ours? We have all been puzzled at stories of people who are found frozen to death with ample funds to pay for heating, clothes or even a new house. How much more inexplicable is the case of those Christians who, faced by need, never draw upon the resources of heaven!

### 3. Heaven is a place of awesome holiness

There is more to heaven than just sheer power; heaven is also a place of holiness. The words 'holy' and 'holiness' are unfamiliar words in a world where it can be truly said that little is held sacred. Behind the concept of 'the holy' is the idea of something so different, so set apart from our own existence and so utterly pure in terms of right or wrong that it is truly awe-inspiring. The descriptions in the Bible of those people who came into contact with God's holiness suggest that the experience was almost totally physically overwhelming (e.g. Exodus 19 and 20; Isaiah 6:1–7). To human beings like ourselves, whose ideas of right and wrong are fairly diluted, there is something almost terrifying about God's total and perfect holiness.

Because heaven is the place, or the dimension, where God is present in all his power, majesty and purity, it is where no sin can enter (see, for example, Isaiah 63:15). Many of the images in the Bible about heaven (its brilliance, its position above us, its white-robed inhabitants) seem designed to reflect this breathtaking holiness. In the Old Testament book of

Nehemiah we read how the prophet Nehemiah hears of trouble in Jerusalem. His response is to pray, and his words tell us a lot about how he viewed heaven:

> When I heard this, I sat down and wept. In fact, for days I mourned, fasted, and prayed to the God of heaven. Then I said, 'O LORD, God of heaven, the great and awesome God who keeps his covenant of unfailing love with those who love him and obey his commands, listen to my prayer! Look down and see me praying night and day for your people Israel. I confess that we have sinned against you. Yes, even my own family and I have sinned! We have sinned terribly by not obeying the commands, laws, and regulations that you gave us through your servant Moses.' (Nehemiah 1:4–7)

His concern in his prayer is that of guilt; he is aware that both he and his people have sinned against God.

Understanding the fact that heaven is holy should produce in us a sense of reverence. If the word 'Father' gives intimacy to our prayers, 'in heaven' should give them humility and reverence. Sadly, in this area the Christian church can swing from one extreme to the other: one generation emphasises God's awesome might so much that people are intimidated by him; the next generation trivialises God so that he is no more than 'my mate up there'. The current fashion is towards a cosy over-familiarity with God. The phrase 'in heaven', with its overtones of overwhelming reality, power and holiness, should make us sit up. God is GOD! God is Father but he is also Lord. And being Lord means that he is in charge, he makes the decisions, he rules. Again we sense the privilege of prayer. The God we pray to is not just a Father; he is Lord of all!

Here too we get the balance of this prayer. By being 'our Father in heaven' God is at the same time both awesome and approachable. If God weren't our Father he would be unapproachable, and if our Father were not the God of heaven, prayer would be futile.

There is also a balance here about the focus of our prayers. If God had defined himself simply as 'Father' we might think that his chief purpose was simply to supply all his children's needs. However, by stating that he is 'in heaven' we are reminded that he is Almighty God and that he exists for his own glory and purposes. It certainly counters any tendency to think of God simply as a form of therapy.

### A shared privilege: *our* Father in heaven

The Lord's Prayer reminds us that we do not begin our prayers with *my* Father but with *our* Father. In fact the words 'I', 'me' and 'mine' do not occur in it; it is 'our' and 'us' all the way through. This is not simply a peculiarity of grammar. The Lord's Prayer is a community prayer; it is the family prayer. It is a reminder to us that we cannot live the Christian faith without considering others. To be a Christian is not just to enter into a relationship between God and us; it is to enter into relationship with other Christians too. Adoption into God's family means that we do not just get a new Father; we also get new brothers and sisters as well.

Of course, if you happen to be in solitary confinement in prison you can still be a Christian and pray this prayer. But to pray this prayer with other Christians has always been the practice of Jesus' followers. Solitary Christianity is not God's pattern for his children. When we pray the Lord's Prayer, whether we pray privately or publicly, we are really coming to God as part of a fellowship of Christians. That fellowship is the church. This phrase 'the church' is often misunderstood. It does not mean a building (as in 'the church by the school') or even some formal organisation of vicars, ministers or pastors; it is the invisible association of all those who have come to know Jesus Christ and have his Spirit in them. Fundamentally the church is never a place but always a people, never a fold but always a flock, never a sacred building but always a believing assembly.

In this sense the church is the ultimate multinational organisation; it is spread all over the world and has branches in almost every town. It cuts across all barriers of age, class, culture, gender and race. When as a Christian you pray, you do not just pray as an individual, you pray as someone who is part of this awesome universal church.

This word 'our' is significant in many ways. It reminds us that we are to be part of a local Christian church, whether it calls itself a church, a chapel, an assembly, a congregation or a community. This is a non-negotiable part of being a Christian. It also reminds us that we come to God, not only as isolated individuals on the planet but as part of this vast buzzing community of those who are in Christ. That ought to be an encouragement if you are in some lonely spot. It certainly makes all the excitement about the World Wide Web seem vastly over-hyped!

Christian fellowship is important for several reasons.

- Fellowship is important for spiritual growth. All Christians are meant to grow in what they know about God and how they live like God. Negatively, we grow by getting rid of old lifestyles, habits and attitudes. Positively, we grow by imitating Jesus Christ and being filled with the Holy Spirit. If we stay in isolation from other Christians it is all too easy to be content with staying the way we are. On our own we can retain bad habits, as well as developing some new ones. In fellowship, God uses other Christians to challenge our behaviour and to give us a prod down the right road. Hebrews 10:24–25 says: 'Think of ways to encourage one another to outbursts of love and good deeds. And let us not neglect our meeting together, as some people do, but encourage and warn each other, especially now that the day of his coming back again is drawing near.' Fellowship is the best soil for spiritual growth.

- Christian fellowship is also important to prevent our spiritual life from being weakened. Although I will discuss the devil in Chapter 7 I think it is important to mention here that his greatest desire is to see the faith of Christians either destroyed or made useless and that one of his most effective strategies is to promote privatised Christianity. When Christians are part of vibrant, sharing, loving fellowships they pose great problems for the devil; together they are too strong for him. But if he can isolate us, separating us off from each other, then he has an opportunity to inflict damage. This is why the devil enjoys a good church split so much; he is guaranteed that there will be lots of isolated Christians whom he can immobilise spiritually. There are real dangers with being a private Christian. Staying with the crowd is a good idea when there are enemies about.

- Sharing the Christian life with others helps keep our faith going. One way of looking at this is to imagine the devil as being someone whose strategy is to lower the temperature of our faith to the point where it is frozen and useless. And it is far easier to reduce the temperature of an individual than a group. Many animals and birds that live in cold climates (penguins, for example) huddle together in groups during winter to maximise their warmth. Another way of looking at the need to be part of a group of Christians is to realise that we all go through highs and lows in our spiritual life. If you are on your own, hitting a deep low may be too tough to bear and your Christian life may take such a battering that it effectively ceases to exist. But if you are with others then you will find that your lows will almost certainly occur when other people have highs and their highs will help carry you through your lows. And when, in turn, your spiritual life improves you will be able to lift others through their own storms.

This little word 'our' is very important. If I were to summarise what it meant I would say that it had two messages for us. The first message is about ourselves. We live today in a very individualistic society. We increasingly tend to live alone, listen to music alone, be entertained alone. The day is not far away when you could spend your entire week working at home, shopping at home, eating at home and amusing yourself at home. All on your own. In such a climate it is easy to see ourselves as the focus of our lives. We need to actively counter that tendency by going out and becoming part of a church. And by being part, I do not mean simply attending; I mean being involved in the life of other Christians. You can quickly lose interest in the church if you have nothing invested. The Christian church is far more than a club. After all, everybody else who has come to know Jesus Christ has the same Father as you. You have a lot in common. You and they (and I) are family.

---

**Floating church members may begin to sink after spending a while in the water.**

---

So let me make a plea: get personally involved with a church. Some families think that the church is like a convention where you send a delegate; and it's usually the mother! Get personally involved and stay involved. Try not to drift from church to church. That does very little good to anybody. Floating church members may begin to sink after spending a while in the water. Don't float, get on board!

The second message for us is about others. *Others matter*. The Christian life is not a solo race with us competing on our own against all the others on the track. Rather it is a team event like a relay race or a football side; we all have to be team players. Or, to switch images, we are an orchestra or a band and so do not always have to play solo. So please pray for others, be concerned for them, grieve over them when they fall and rejoice with them when they achieve. This involvement with others is not just for our good; it is also for the good of the church. Whether we like it or not, churches are fellowships of interlinked individuals. When you think of church, you should think of 'us' and 'we', not 'me' and 'them'.

So how are we to think of ourselves? There are two extreme stands taken on what it is to be a Christian. One viewpoint says

that Christians are primarily individuals and life is a race that is
to be run. With this view we must work hard to ensure that we
personally run our own race of faith as best we can. There are
many Bible verses that would support this view (e.g.
1 Corinthians 9:24–27; Philippians 3:13–14). The opposing
view is that we are all part of a collective body to the extent that
we really no longer exist as individuals; we are instead all part
of the body of Christ. Interestingly enough, there would be
Bible verses to support this too (e.g. 1 Corinthians 12:12, 27;
Ephesians 2:13–16). The truth is that both views are partially
right. We *are* individuals, and we can only come to Christ on
our own. We cannot be converted by anyone else's decision,
whether they are our parents, our minister or our friend. Yet
we are not just individuals; we must also be part of the communal body, the church.


## PRACTICAL IMPLICATIONS

### Think about how you pray

Imagine you were told that tomorrow you were going to meet
some incredibly important person such as the Queen, the
Prime Minister or the President of the USA for a discussion.
Wouldn't you spend much of the next 24 hours thinking about
what you were going to say? You'd probably write down some
thoughts on what you wanted to speak about, rewrite them
several times to get the words just right and then memorise
them so that when you had the opportunity to speak, you
could say the right thing. And as the time of the meeting got
nearer you would probably find yourself starting to get

nervous. Does your hair look OK? Should you have bought new clothes?

The irony is that all too often we come to prayer with God, the King of heaven, without any thought at all. Now don't get me wrong. I am not suggesting that we lie awake all night wondering what to say in our prayers. That would be to deny the fact that God is our Father. There is a freedom for us to come into God's presence, and if trouble should come upon us suddenly, then we should get on and pray about it. Our Father well understands that his children may have sudden crises. In fact there are some pretty urgent prayers in the Bible (e.g. Nehemiah 2:4–5; Acts 7:59–60). But ordinarily if we were to think of who it is we are talking to in prayer, we wouldn't rush in with too many words. It is a good rule to think about who you are meeting with in prayer and to think about the awesome privilege you enjoy in being able to talk to God. Treating a meeting with Almighty God as a routine thing or, even worse, a necessary duty seems somewhat disrespectful.

## Think about how you live

The significance of this opening phrase of the Lord's Prayer for how we live is astonishing. Let me just list a few of the implications of us calling God 'our Father in heaven'.

It should give us a *sense of worth*. It is easy to feel worthless today when our world seems to say through the media that only the rich, powerful and beautiful have significance. Yet if you can indeed call God 'Father' then what you are saying is, '*I* am God's child.' Think about that. It means you are loved, special and significant. You may consider yourself nothing, you may imagine you are unlovely and unloved, but if you are in the position to pray this prayer then you are a much-loved child of God. And with being a child of God comes many other privileges, such as being heirs of God, belonging to a kingdom of priests and being a member of God's holy nation (Romans 8:17; 1 Peter 2:9). You may need to think this almost daily as you pray. You may definitely need to remind yourself about this when, for example, you are faced with something that implies that unless you wear particular clothing or own certain possessions, you are nothing. Those who can pray this prayer are God's children and there are no riches or influence in the whole world that can be traded for that!

---

**God wants every single one of his children to be his ambassador and representative.**

---

It should give us a *sense of significance*. I've heard it said that one of the main problems with most Christians today is that deep down, where it matters most, they don't really believe what they say they believe. For many people this is true about prayer. Let me ask you a very personal question. Do you live out your life in a way that reflects the fact that you regularly talk with the Maker of the universe? When you stride into work or school in the morning, does what you say and do reflect the fact that, probably within the last hour or so, you have spent some time talking with someone who, as God of heaven, has made the whole universe? And that you had the conversation on the basis of a child with their loving father? If you really believe it, then it ought to show in your life. And of course as God's child you not only have significance, you have purpose.

God wants every single one of his children to be his ambassador and representative.

It should give us a *sense of responsibility*. Precisely because we are God's ambassadors we need to be careful how we live. God has given us the right to be his sons and daughters; we now need to live up to that extraordinary privilege. How do we do that? In short, we are to imitate Jesus Christ. Jesus lived on earth not just in order to die for us but also to set out plainly for us how we are to live. The way he lived is the way we should live. We need to remember the encouraging truth that living the Christian life is not entirely dependent upon our own strength and power. After all, which of us could hope to imitate Jesus on our own? God has given all his children the Holy Spirit to help us become more like Jesus, the prototype of the children of God.

So positively, we need to do all we can to live like Christ if we claim the God of heaven as our Father. In a negative sense, we must be careful that we do not let how we live reflect badly on our heavenly Father. We must pray and struggle against sin to ensure that our lives never bring discredit to our heavenly Father. The family honour is at stake!

Having God as our heavenly Father is a tremendous privilege and a responsibility. If we even partially understand what it is to have been made a son or daughter of God then much of what it means to live our lives by God's priorities is already plain.

## QUESTIONS

- If you were to imagine a drama sketch to show how you pray, which of these would it be most like? A slave bowing before a master? A pupil before a headteacher? A soldier standing before a general? A child sitting next to his father or mother?

- There are two errors for us to fall into with God: over-familiarity or fear. How can you strike the right balance?
- As a Christian, do you think of yourself as being an individual or as being part of a family? The dangers of being a lone Christian are fairly obvious, but are there problems with seeing yourself only as part of a church?
- What is the difference between a childish faith and a child-like faith?
- Do you show a family resemblance to your Father? Is acquiring a better resemblance to God something that is an absolute priority for you?
- Is the privilege of having God as our Father in heaven one of those things of which it can be said 'use it or lose it'?
- How might you apply this phrase to a Christian
  - who was bereaved?
  - who faced financial ruin?
  - who had been badly disfigured in an accident?
- What would you say to someone who by their own admission was not a Christian but liked to use this prayer?

# 3
# Praise

*Hallowed be thy name.*
(Traditional)

*May your name be honoured.*
(New Living Translation)

We can now move to the first petition in the Lord's Prayer –
that God's name be honoured or hallowed.

## PUTTING GOD FIRST

In organising the prayer the way Jesus does, he sets out the
right priority for all praying. It is all too easy for us to leap into
prayer with a long and urgent shopping list of requests: 'Lord,
sort out Dave's job!', 'Our Father, help us find the cat!' and so
on. Jesus does not say that such prayers are wrong. But what
he does say is that they must take second place. Our prayers
should first of all start with God and with God's priorities.

But why does God make it a priority that we put him first?
The reason is that to pray this way is to get things in the right
perspective, indeed the only perspective in which prayer can
function. Quite simply, God is *God* – wonderful, awesome and

majestic beyond measure. Any prayer that does not start off with recognising the might, power and glory of God is totally distorted.

Let me make two points here.

## 1. Putting God first is the right thing to do

By putting God first we are worshipping him and praising him as the Lord and Master of the universe. The old hymn 'Crown him with many crowns' not only has a great tune but also a great message. It is also a wonderfully helpful image. What we are doing in this first petition is crowning God in our hearts and renewing our allegiance to him as our King. Of course God already is King – our prayers do not make him any more of a king than he already is. What we are doing here is celebrating that fact and reminding ourselves of the great truth that God is Lord over all. Praise is the only right thing to do; it is the natural and appropriate response to thinking about God.

When we come to God, to put him first is to acknowledge the most important truth in the universe: the fact that God rules over all. Not to put him first suggests that we have not really understood who God is. That is a very poor way to begin praying.

By putting God first what we are actually doing in prayer is reminding ourselves of what is reality. The world around us continually tries to persuade us that God is insignificant and unimportant. In contrast what we are doing by following Jesus' pattern of prayer is simply reorienting our world the right way. We are seeing things as they really are; we are getting the picture straight.

So we praise God simply because of who he is. Justice demands that his glory receives a response of praise from us. God deserves praise.

---

### 'Little God, big problems; big God, little problems.'

---

Yet praise is also good for us. The purpose of praise is to give God glory; the fact that it is good for us is simply a bonus. Getting the perspective right on God is vital. Imagine, for example, that you face a crisis at work. On the other side of the world the owners of the company you work for are planning to close down your factory. It all looks hopeless. Now if you start praying to God using the pattern Jesus gave in the Lord's Prayer, then the first thing you have to do is to forget your own problems and focus on God and on his majesty and his desires. The result is that when you eventually get to the crisis at work you'll come to it with the awareness that you are talking about it to the one person in the universe who can really do something about it. In contrast, if you come to God and blurt out your problems straight away, you may easily get the feeling that they are bigger than God. There is an old saying that is well worth remembering: 'Little God, big problems; big God, little problems'.

## 2. Putting ourselves first is the wrong thing to do

The other side of the coin is that if we put ourselves before God and his desires, we turn our faith on its head. We make our needs more important than God's kingdom, righteousness or glory. We end up praying that we can get home from work early instead of asking that some appalling African war is ended. What have we done? I'll tell you: we have become self-centred. God is a selfless God and he wants us to be selfless too.

With prayers that are just personal shopping lists we can soon come to perceive God as someone who exists only for our benefit. If we keep on, then very soon we will have turned God into someone (or something) who is nothing more than a means of supplying our wants. This is something God cannot allow. Everybody has met children who have been thoroughly spoiled by over-indulgent parents giving them whatever they want, whether it is good for them or not. In the end it ruins the relationship. God is the perfect parent; he is not going to allow that to happen to us.

God wants to have a deep personal relationship with us and such a relationship can only take place when we treat him as more than just a spiritual Santa Claus to give us what we want. I think this is a point we need to consider very carefully. In today's consumer society it is all too easy to think of God as merely the boss of the great shopping mall in the sky. Putting God and his priorities first in our praying reminds us of the right order of things. Our relativist consumer society tells us that God is what we want him to be. The truth is that God's character, will and holiness do not change.

## HONOURING GOD'S NAME

The first clause in the Lord's Prayer states, 'May your name be honoured' (or 'hallowed'). What does that mean? Why God's *name* and why *honoured*?

## God's name

What does 'God's name' mean? Well, at its most basic level God's name is equivalent to God himself. To say, 'God, let your name be honoured,' is the same as saying, 'God, may *you* be honoured.' However, there is even more to it than this.

In our culture your name is simply the string of letters that is used to call you, and if someone were to say to you, 'May your name be honoured,' it would sound very strange. Mind you, we know what it is like to have our names dishonoured; and you do hear people protesting that their name has been dragged through the mud. Yet to really understand this part of the Lord's Prayer we need to be aware of the meaning of names in the culture of the Bible. For people around the Mediterranean then (and many people in that area today) their personal name had meaning; it stood for everything they were. That is why there are so many comments in the Old Testament (often clarified in footnotes in our Bibles) on the meaning of the names of people and places. For example, in Genesis 3:20 we are told that '*Eve* sounds like a Hebrew term that means "to give life"'. Sometimes God gives people a new name when their life changes. 'Abram' for example becomes 'Abraham' and 'Jacob' becomes 'Israel' (Genesis 17:5; 32:28). The old name will no longer do.

One of the great themes of the Old Testament is the name of God. To the Israelites God was not an impersonal force or an unknown God. He had a name (Exodus 3:15). That name, which was pronounced Yahweh, is what lies behind the phrase 'The LORD' that we find nearly 7,000 times in the Old

Testament of our English Bibles. In Exodus 3:14 God makes a great statement about who he is: 'I AM THE ONE WHO ALWAYS IS' or 'I AM WHO I AM', and the word 'Yahweh' seems to be a shortened version of this; effectively 'I AM' . So not only did God's people know God's personal name; it reminded them that he was the great unchanging one whose promises they could trust. Incidentally, the word Jehovah is an earlier attempt at pronouncing Yahweh.

Throughout the Old Testament God uses other names for himself, each of which reveals more of who he is. Let me just list some of the names God uses. There are about 15 names that involve compound forms of the name Yahweh. Some of the most important are perhaps:

- *Yahweh yir'eh*: 'The LORD Will Provide' (Genesis 22:14).
- *Yahweh nissi*: 'The LORD Is My Banner' (Exodus 17:15).
- *Yahweh shalom*: 'The LORD Is Peace' (Judges 6:24).
- *Yahweh tsebaoth*: 'The LORD Almighty' or 'The LORD of Hosts' (1 Samuel 4:4). (The idea here seems to be that God is the Lord of all heaven's angelic armies.)

Then there are the other titles of God, such as:

- *Shepherd* (e.g. Genesis 49:24; Psalm 23:1; Isaiah 40:11).
- *King* (Psalm 95:3).
- *Judge* (Genesis 18:25).
- *Redeemer* (Isaiah 44:24).
- *Warrior* (Exodus 15:3).
- *Rock* (Psalm 18:2).
- *Glory* (Exodus 16:7; Psalm 104:31).

- *The Holy One* (Isaiah 1:4).
- *The Mighty One* (Genesis 49:24).

I could add to these all the adjectives that God applies to himself such as loving, holy, merciful, fair, good, righteous and so on. And, of course, I could supplement these further with other titles that occur in the New Testament.

It is important we realise that these names are not just seen as the basis of Biblical Trivial Pursuits or the components of obscure worship songs. The fact is that they are profoundly helpful. These words and phrases are all titles that God has said can apply to him. So we can say in our praying, 'O God who is our Shepherd,' or, 'O God who is our Rock,' and expect, in faith, that he will live up to that title. Now I don't know about you, but there are many times in my life when I need a shepherd to lead me, a warrior to fight for me, a rock to give me support, and these titles (and there are more) are how God describes himself.

So it is worth remembering that there are riches in God's name.

## Honouring God's name as holy

God's name includes all that he is and all that he has said he is. But what exactly does it mean for God's name to be 'hallowed' or 'honoured'?

The word 'hallow' is not a common word today, which is presumably why the New Living Translation uses the word 'honour'. The old word is useful and worth thinking about because to hallow something really means 'to set it apart as holy or sacred'. This leads us on to something that needs discussing because it is often overlooked today: the unfamiliar idea of holiness.

While the concept of holiness is one that is strange to us in the modern secular West, to the Jews the fact that God was holy was something that lay at the centre of their faith. In fact God was not only holy, he was, according to Isaiah 6:3, 'Holy, Holy, Holy'. Therefore you gave God enormous respect that bordered on what we would call fear. That is why there is so much in the Old Testament about clean and unclean food, priests, sacrifices and rituals. For a Jew, God was so holy that only people who were themselves physically pure in every way and who were separated from anything that might be unclean, could approach him. The result is that ideas of clean and unclean, holy and impure, run across almost every page of the Old Testament.

This whole Old Testament system of ritual cleanliness was fulfilled and completely revised by God coming, in the flesh, as Jesus. In Christ, wonder of wonders, God became one of us, lived among us and ate with us. In fact, Jesus went out of his way to touch (or let himself be touched by) those who were considered to be ritually unclean, such as lepers, women contaminated by diseases that made them impure, or even non-Jews. Following on from Jesus' teaching (e.g. Mark 7:17–23) it was not long before his followers dismantled virtually all the Old Testament rituals on diet and worship (see Acts 15). For the Christian, holiness was no longer something solely to do with external physical purity (what you ate and who you touched), but was to be a matter of inner purity and cleansing through the Holy Spirit.

In making this verdict, I think, of course, that Jesus' follow-

ers were right. Yet one side-effect of their decision is that
because we have lost the physical, daily reminders that God is
holy, there is always a risk that we minimise the holiness of God.
To the practising Jew, every detail of life, from the kosher food
to how they dressed, reflected these ideas of being clean and
separate from the world; they were regular and inescapable

---

**We have lost the physical, daily reminders that
God is holy.**

---

memory aids that God himself was totally separate. We need to
keep reminding ourselves that God is holy. This is a particular
problem in our culture where we have tended to downplay or
even ignore the idea of holiness. If we treat God as someone
who is common or ordinary, in doing so we devalue both the
awesome moral purity of God and the astonishing work of the
cross in making us clean before him. We need somehow to
recover the truth of God's holiness. Have you ever been in some
important meeting with people you are desperately trying to
impress, only to realise that there is a prominent soup stain on
your shirt or blouse and that *everyone* is looking at it? Definitely
one of those 'if only the ground could open up and swallow me'
moments! Yet how infinitely more dreadful it would be to stand
in the glare of a holy, pure God with all the spots of dirt on our
souls exposed! That's what God's holiness means. And that's
why the forgiveness Jesus offers is so wonderful: we have access
to God through one who has covered over our sins. We need to
deepen our awareness of both God's holiness and Jesus' forgiveness. If we emphasise the holiness alone we will find God
too terrifying to approach; if we emphasise the forgiveness alone

then the danger is that we will take God for granted. We need to know more about both his holiness and his forgiveness.

When we pray 'May your name be hallowed' we need to remember that God is holy. If you use the version with 'honoured' then that's fine, as long as you remember that it is not just honoured in the sense of 'God's a really good bloke' but honoured in the sense of holy.

Associated with this idea of God's name is the whole concept of authority. In biblical times your name was linked with your authority and status. For instance, you might send a slave on an errand, and although the slave would have no real status of their own they could ask for things in your name. The more authority or power you had, the faster your slave would be served. This idea is familiar to us – anyone who has been sent on an errand by their boss has come across it. However, the important thing is that God's name gives us, as Christians, the only authority we have and actually the only authority that is worth anything. If someone preaches in Jesus' name, it means they do it (or they ought to do it) not on their own but under his authority. If someone prays for healing in Jesus' name, it means they do it under his authority. When we pray for something (as in 'Lord, we ask all these things in Jesus' name'), what we are saying is, 'Lord, we ask for these things under your name's power and authority'. It is as if we are writing the order for something to be done and then getting God to put his signature of authorisation against it. This prayer then is that God's name will be recognised as having weight and authority and will not be dishonoured.

So to pray 'May God's name be honoured' is to pray that more and more people on earth would recognise and submit to the authority and rule of God. Every time someone refuses to commit some act of corruption because of their conscience or their knowledge of God, then God's name is honoured. Whenever someone repents and comes to faith in Jesus, God's name is honoured.

Praising God is honouring or hallowing God's name. But praising God is not just singing a few worship songs or hymns to him. It is to treat God, in word, thought and action, as the unique awesomely holy God that he is. By praising him, either in our prayers, our songs, our words or our actions, we honour his name by setting him above everything else.

## PRACTICAL IMPLICATIONS

*Practically* what does it mean for God's name to be made holy? It might help us to understand this expression better if we think about how we might express it in a negative way. To do that would be to pray something like, 'Lord, may your name not be dishonoured; may your name not be shamed or dragged down into the dirt.' So as we think about the implications of this phrase, we need to think about both the negative and positive of honouring God's name.

### Think about how you pray

This opening petition of the Lord's Prayer asks all of us an awkward and uncomfortable question. Do we treat God as holy? We may pray for his name to be honoured in the world, but is it honoured in our prayer life? I realise he is our Father, but have we let that totally obliterate the concept of his holiness?

How many of our prayers (and I do not exempt myself from criticism here) really treat God as being awesomely holy? Next time you have just finished praying, run over what passed through your mind during prayer. Imagine that some mental video had been taken of what you thought and said. You will realise that for at least some of the time your mind wandered all over the place; some of your prayer made no sense whatsoever and a sense of God's presence was absent for a large percentage of the time. It is not just in our private prayers that this happens. It's amazing what your mind can turn to during church prayers or even singing hymns or worship songs.

There are three possible reactions to this recognition that much of our praying is poor, and two of them are badly wrong.

The first wrong reaction is apathy. 'Oh well,' someone may say, 'it's just one of those things. I guess I'm just not a born pray-er.' That is potentially very dangerous.

The second wrong reaction, and perhaps the commonest, is despair. Crushed by our inadequacy, we begin to think that we are total failures and possibly not even Christians. Such feelings are probably from the devil. As we will see in Chapter 7, the devil has a strategy for inflicting guilt, discouragement and

---

**Pray about how you pray.**

---

despair. It might be encouraging to think of the conversation between an earthly parent and his small son or daughter. The child may well speak with faulty grammar, mumbling, lapses of concentration and statements that are quite illogical. But what loving parent would be harsh with them over it?

The third and best reaction to recognising your failings is to say sorry to God and to seek encouragement to go forward. You might want to pray about how you pray and to ask God to help you to pray more effectively. This reminds me of the person who asked me, 'What shall I do? I'm finding praying really hard.'

I said, 'Pray.'

The person then insisted, 'But you're not hearing me. Praying is what I'm finding hard.'

I replied, 'You need to pray.'

Perseverance in prayer, when it is hard, is vital.

We can also undo a lot of the good of prayer by what we do afterwards. Imagine, for instance, that in your praying you have a great time praising God and get really excited about how he supplies all our needs. Then you say 'Amen', and go and read the mail that has just come. One letter is from the bank, pointing out that you have exceeded your credit limit. Now if your reaction is to despair, shout at everybody and *not at all* to remember that God is your heavenly Father who cares for you, then you must really ask yourself how deep and how real that prayer was. It certainly didn't connect to what you feel is the real world. If on the other hand, however, you take a deep breath and say, 'Well thank you, Lord, for the lesson I just learned in prayer. I need it now,' that's another matter. In that case your prayer has done something.

In John 17:11 Jesus refers to God as 'Holy Father'. Those two words hold the balance of what God should be to us. He wants to be close to us and unapproachably distant; to be affectionate and awesome; to be Loving Father and Holy Judge.

## Think about how you live

It is not enough to pray this prayer. We need to live it out. Prayer and practice must be linked. Our prayers set the pattern of our lives. Remember those war films, where the heroes sit in the briefing hall, are told about their mission, issued with maps, reminded of their duty, warned of the hazards and then sent on their way? This prayer is a bit like that. It is the basis, or it should be the basis, upon which the rest of our lives are built. Incidentally, that is why most people try to find time to do their praying in the morning before the day starts. Of course that may not be possible, but if you can manage it, it's helpful to have spent some time with God *before* you are faced with the bills, the traffic jams and your colleague's hangover. A great nineteenth-century missionary, Hudson Taylor, said, 'It's a good idea to tune your instruments before the concert begins.' Remember that every day we will be given an opportunity to honour or dishonour God's name.

In the Old Testament God speaks through the prophet Amos to denounce praise without a matching practice:

> I hate all your show and pretence – the hypocrisy of your religious festivals and solemn assemblies. I will not accept your burnt offerings and grain offerings. I won't even notice all your choice peace offerings. Away with your hymns of praise! They are only noise to my ears. I will not listen to your music, no matter how lovely it is. Instead, I want to see a mighty flood of justice, a river of righteous living that will never run dry. (Amos 5:21–24)

We need to remember that words of praise without appropriate actions are just a noise to God.

One rather troubling question should arise if you think about what it means to pray for God's name to be honoured: what are you *personally* doing about it? If you pray, 'Lord, glorify your name! Clean up crime in this town, convert my neighbours and please save those people in Nepal!' then shouldn't you try and do something about it? Now of course you may, by reason of age, illness or poverty, be unable to do anything other than pray. But to the rest of us the frank question must be asked: Are we putting our time, money and energy where our mouths are?

Imagine one winter's morning you find that there has been an overnight snowfall; three or maybe four inches of snow blocks your drive. The main road has, however, been cleared and you have to get to work. All you have to do is clear a way for your car. How would you feel if, as you sweated away at shovelling snow, a group of fit and healthy lads gathered around you, watched you intently and made comments like this?

'Only six feet to go.'

'Just think how good the exercise is for you.'

'We are with you in spirit.'

'You're doing a really super job.'

'It'll melt if you leave it long enough.' (That's the optimist.)

'Looks like more snow on the way.' (That's the pessimist.)

'It will move faster if you put more on the shovel.'

You would soon get very exasperated and might easily end up suggesting, in the politest possible manner of course, that either they give you a helping hand or they clear off. I suggest that for a lot of us our prayer is like this. We want to be spectators not players; civilians not combatants; critics not performers. We say, 'Lord, let your name be honoured in Central Asia,' but under our breath, in a voice so low that we think God won't hear it, we say, '. . . and get someone else to do it.' We are bystanders, ever ready for praise, theological reflection or giving a vote of thanks to our heroic missionary/minister/social worker/Sunday school teacher/evangelist/catering team, but somehow always absent when it comes to signing up. Remember: worship and work; praise and practice go together.

A few years ago it was suggested that vast mirrors be unfurled in space to reflect the sun's light and heat to the regions of Canada and Siberia that in winter are in almost permanent frozen darkness. It is a wonderful image for how we are to live as Christians. We are to be those who, by our lives, take the light of God and reflect it into the dark frozen places of the world. That, it seems to me, is what it really means to honour God.

It seems to me completely clear that if we ask God to honour or hallow his name, we ought to say immediately after our prayers, 'And so, Lord, what can I *personally* do about that?'

God's answer may well be one that will cost us our time, our money or far more. But what we have to remember is that when it came to saving us, God did not sit on his hands in heaven, wishing us well. He became one of us and, extending his hands, let himself be crucified.

Do you see why praying, *real* praying, is about the riskiest, most exciting life-changing thing you can do?

I wonder if that is why so many of us only pretend to do it.

## QUESTIONS

- How can I bring honour to God
  - at home?
  - at work?
  - in my community?
  - in what I do in life?
- How can I bring dishonour to God
  - at home?
  - at work?
  - in my community?
  - in what I do in life?
- How can a church honour God's name? How can it dishonour God's name?
- You are on a walk when someone, admiring the wonderful view before you, says, 'Nature did a nice bit of work here.' Are they honouring God? What should you say?
- Which of the following would be ways of honouring God as a Christian man or woman in the business world?
  - Having a Bible text over your desk.
  - Paying your taxes.
  - Refusing to listen to dirty jokes.
  - Selling a good fair product for a fair price.
  - Forbidding the misuse of Christ's name.

# 4
# Purpose

*Thy kingdom come; thy will be done, on earth as it is in heaven.*
(Traditional)

*May your Kingdom come soon.*
*May your will be done here on earth,*
*just as it is in heaven.*
(New Living Translation)

There are two big questions in life. The first one is intensely personal: What am I here for? The second is more universal: Where is the world going? This clause in the Lord's Prayer addresses both questions.

'What am I here for?' sums up all those speculations we have about the meaning of life. How we live and how we make our decisions depends on how we answer this question. In fact when people do not believe in God or the Bible, this is such an uncomfortable question that they tend to dodge it. Instead they just live for the present, trying to push to one side any thought of the future with its looming shadow of death.

In 1776 the American Declaration of Independence stated that among humanity's 'unalienable rights' were 'life, liberty and the pursuit of happiness'. This has now become the guiding principle of most people; life is the hunt for happiness and personal pleasure. To this end we seek gratification through shopping, sex, food, leisure and holidays. And yet, by general admission, it is all so unsatisfying. Is this, you ask yourself at the end of another long day, why I work? Just so I can go shopping to buy things? Have I no more purpose in life than simply to be a consumer? What happened to my hopes, my desires, my destiny?

'Where is the world going?' is the second great question. It may be a less personal question but it is one that is no less troubling. We look back at the past, gaze at our present world and peer anxiously into the unknown future. There used to be hope, but it is hard to find optimists any more. Is the world's destiny ecological destruction? Will civilisation end in some war of mutual nuclear or biological destruction? Will we wake one day to find out that metallic replacements with silicon brains have decided that it's their time to run the show? Or will some lumbering asteroid collide with us, wiping everything out so that evolution can begin all over again? So many of today's films play on these fears of the dark side of the future with their plots of meteorite impacts, alien invasions, computers running wild, ecological disasters and unstoppable plagues. When the script of history's great drama is left to us, it is easy to fear the worst.

This phrase of the Lord's Prayer, 'May your Kingdom come soon. May your will be done here on earth, just as it is in heaven', and all that lies behind it, deals with both our purpose and this world's purpose. As such, it is worth thinking about very carefully.

Some people consider that asking for 'God's kingdom to

come' and for 'his will to be done' are two separate petitions. Certainly if you do, the Lord's Prayer acquires an elegant symmetry: three petitions for what God wants, followed by three for what we need. Yet, as we shall see, distinguishing between God's kingdom and God's will is far from easy. In fact it is easier to treat them as one single petition. I am encouraged to do this by Luke's version of the Lord's Prayer, which simply says, 'May your kingdom come soon.'

## WHAT DID JESUS MEAN BY 'THE KINGDOM OF GOD'?

Even the hastiest flick through the pages of the first three gospels (Matthew, Mark and Luke) will show lots of references to 'the kingdom' or 'the kingdom of God'. Matthew, writing to believers from a Jewish background who would have been uneasy about using the name of God, uses an alternative, 'the kingdom of heaven', which means the same thing. The kingdom of God was clearly a central part of Jesus' teaching. In fact Jesus opens his public ministry with this announcement. At the start of Mark's Gospel we read that after John the Baptist was arrested, 'Jesus went to Galilee to preach God's Good News. "At last the time has come!" he announced. "The Kingdom of God is near! Turn from your sins and believe this Good News!"' (Mark 1:14–15). But what did he mean by it?

The Old Testament has very little to say about God's kingdom but a lot to say about God as King and even more to say about God's rule. The LORD was the real King of Israel (Psalm 47:2; 99:1; 145:1; Isaiah 6:5). He had, however, allowed a series of human monarchs to act as kings of Israel under him. With a few exceptions, notably David (and he had failed morally), they had been rather dismal failures, and with the conquest of Jerusalem in 586 BC and the exile to Babylon, the line of kings had ended. However, the prophets had spoken of a future Ruler, the Messiah. Descended from David, this mysterious figure (human but also Godlike) would be the ultimate King and would rule the world from Jerusalem (see, for example, Isaiah 9:7; 11:1–16; 24:23). By the time of Jesus the Jewish people had had centuries of heavy-handed oppression by foreigners and there was now a widespread hunger for both God's King and God's kingdom. However, much of the population seems to have seen the ideas of the King and the kingdom in very physical and nationalistic terms. Many of them believed that when the Messiah came, there would be a new (and expanded) geographical state of Israel and proper worship would be established in the Temple. As much as the idea of such a Messiah excited the Jewish community, it alarmed the Roman ruling powers.

It is vital to be aware of this popular view in order to be able to understand Jesus' teaching. Much of what Jesus said and did seems to have been done with two purposes in mind. On the one hand he wanted to make it plain that he was indeed God's King and that he brought with him the kingdom, but on the other he wanted to make it equally plain that neither his kingship nor the kingdom that he offered was what so many of the Jews longed for and the Romans dreaded.

From the teaching of John the Baptist and (far more importantly) Jesus, we can isolate six points about the kingdom.

## 1. The kingdom is God's *dominion*

Perhaps the most important thing that Jesus taught about the kingdom of God is that it is not a place, a country or any sort of geographical location. Unlike this world's kingdoms and republics, it appears on no maps, issues no passports and maintains no embassies. The kingdom is wherever God is King. Jesus made this point when the Pharisees asked him, ' "When will the Kingdom of God come?" Jesus replied, "The Kingdom of God isn't ushered in with visible signs. You won't be able to say, 'Here it is!' or 'It's over there!' For the Kingdom of God is among you" ' (Luke 17:20–21).

Not surprisingly, the nature of the kingdom came up when Jesus was brought before Pontius Pilate, the representative of the Roman Empire. To his questioning Jesus replied, 'I am not an earthly king. If I were, my followers would have fought when I was arrested by the Jewish leaders. But my Kingdom is not of this world' (John 18:36). In short, the kingdom is not a nation; it is wherever God's rule is accepted in the lives of men and women.

What does this mean? Imagine, for example, someone becoming a Christian one weekend. On the Friday they are (although they may not realise it) an enemy of God. They run their life their way, under their priorities, and their whole existence is governed by one rule: '*my* will be done'. During the next two days, however, they surrender to God and recognise Jesus as their Lord and Saviour. In making that decision they have said to Jesus, 'Let *your* will be done, not mine.' They are therefore allowing God to enter their lives through his Holy Spirit, and in doing so they have become part of the kingdom of God.

Although what has happened is an extraordinary transaction involving the birth of a new creature, it might easily have taken place with almost no physical, measurable changes. As the new believer leaves for work on Monday there would be little obvious external change to mark this transformation. No new

---

**Membership of the kingdom is never a private matter.**

---

flag now flies over their house. Coming into the kingdom of God by submitting to God's dominion begins with an invisible operation. Nevertheless, underneath the unchanged surface, the believer has now acquired a whole new set of loyalties and priorities, although they may not have realised this. Although the new birth may have been private and not visible, the changed priorities should soon start to show. Membership of the kingdom is never a private matter because citizens of the kingdom are expected to work towards the kingdom's concerns, such as truth, love and justice. If Jesus has indeed taken charge of our lives, then our new ownership should soon be apparent.

The Bible is clear that precisely because God's kingdom is about dominion, it is at war with Satan in a spiritual conflict. Across the planet, invisible to us, warfare rages between the opposing kingdoms. The apostle Paul says in Colossians 1:13–14, 'For he has rescued us from the one who rules in the kingdom of darkness, and he has brought us into the Kingdom of his dear Son. God has purchased our freedom with his blood and has forgiven all our sins.'

The Bible speaks little of these battles (but see, for example, Daniel 10:12–13; Ephesians 6:12; Revelation 1:7–9) and much of our speculation on this matter is probably both unwarranted and unwise. We need to be aware that part of the establishing of the kingdom of God is about God's power overthrowing Satan. Indeed, Jesus makes his own exorcisms proof that he is bringing in the kingdom: 'But if I am casting out demons by the power of God, then the Kingdom of God has arrived among you' (Luke 11:20). Every believer needs to realise two things in this regard: first, all followers of Jesus are faced by hostile evil forces, and second, through Jesus Christ's victory on the cross the power of the devil has been broken and his ultimate fate sealed. Colossians 2:13–15 speaks encouragingly to us of this victory:

> You were dead because of your sins and because your sinful nature was not yet cut away. Then God made you alive with Christ. He forgave all our sins. He cancelled the record that contained the charges against us. He took it and destroyed it by nailing it to Christ's cross. In this way, God disarmed the evil rulers and authorities. He shamed them publicly by his victory over them on the cross of Christ.

The devil's final, complete and utter defeat is assured.

We need also to remember that this kingdom is God's, not ours. Before we pray 'may your kingdom come' we must be willing to pray 'may my kingdom go'. The kingdom is designed, made and implemented to God's specification; our duty is to submit to it. Sometimes we are tempted to think that it is God's task to back our projects or dreams so that when we pray 'your kingdom come' what we are really praying is '*our* kingdom come'. This is a mistake. As this phrase in the Lord's

Prayer reminds us, our absolute priority is for God's will to be done in our life.

At the time of the first Moon landing, just at the breathless moment when the lunar module was about to descend to the Moon's surface, there was a phone call to NASA. The caller was apologetic, but said that they had to go shopping, so could the landing be delayed? It is an amusing story, but how much more foolish and arrogant is it to ask God to shape his plans around us?

This idea that the kingdom of God is God's rule or dominion can help us to understand why there is the phrase 'on earth as it is in heaven' included in this petition. That clause does not simply apply to God's will being done; it also applies to God's name being glorified and to God's kingdom coming. It is a plea that this troubled earth will soon come to have the same harmonious state as that of heaven. Heaven, of course, is already totally under God's dominion; there all the angels and archangels are already joyfully doing God's will, and by doing so, glorifying his name. In the dimension of heaven, unlike on earth, there is no rebellion; in heaven God's kingdom reigns perfectly and gloriously. There God's will is done completely. The Christian's hope and prayer is that sooner rather than later God's perfect rule will be brought into this world.

Some people, especially those with experience of totalitarian states, can quite understandably feel unhappy with all this language of power, control and command. Think instead in musical terms and imagine that every created thing in heaven and earth is a member of a choir or an orchestra. In heaven everybody is playing and singing harmoniously in tune under God's direction to create the most awesome and wonderful music. However, on rebellious earth the sounds are very different. Here instrument plays against instrument, voices sing and shout in different keys, and the harsh, discordant noise almost totally drowns out the few voices and instruments that are struggling to play heaven's great tune. This petition then is simply that one day all on this earth will be in harmony with the great song of heaven.

---

**The issue of the kingdom comes down to whether we accept Jesus Christ as King.**

---

In fact, because the kingdom is really about how we accept God's rule, then the issue of the kingdom comes down to whether we accept Jesus Christ as King. For Jesus is inseparable from the kingdom. To accept Jesus Christ is to accept the kingdom; to reject Jesus Christ is to reject the kingdom.

## 2. The kingdom is *dynamic*

Many of Jesus' parables point out that there is a tremendous inherent power to the kingdom. For example, the kingdom operates in the way buried seeds mysteriously put out shoots and leaves on their own (Mark 4:26–29). There is an inner dimension to the kingdom.

This dynamic power is shown in the way that although this kingdom starts as something small, it can grow enormously. Seed sown on good soil produces a rich harvest (Matthew 13:8, 23). The tiny mustard seed produces a tree in which birds can shelter (Matthew 13:31–32) and a tiny fragment of yeast affects all the dough when making bread (Matthew 13:33).

The lesson here is that although the kingdom may appear small and insignificant (and even invisible), it is powerful and unstoppable. We must never underestimate the kingdom's power. The greatest illustration of this is the Christian church itself, which although not the same thing as the kingdom, is a product of the kingdom. From the most inauspicious of starts, a mismatched group of ex-fishermen, former tax-collectors and their friends, with no obvious resources, took on the entire Roman Empire and won. Now, 20 centuries later, the modern Western world is one that has been shaped by Christianity, and today followers of Jesus are found right across the globe. The mustard seed has indeed grown into a mighty tree.

### 3. The kingdom is a *delight*

According to Jesus (e.g. Luke 8:1) the kingdom of God is good news. In fact, a number of parables make the point that the kingdom is something so wonderful that we can only desire and long for it. Jesus frequently uses images of banquets, parties and wine drinking to describe heaven (Matthew 22:1–14; 25:1–13; Mark 14:25; Luke 14:15–24).

The lesson here is that the delight of the kingdom is so great that it is not to be missed. Our response to the kingdom ought to be appropriate to God's great extravagance. We should take up the invitation immediately. What foolishness it would be to lose out on God's joyful kingdom!

Equally this affects our attitude to sharing the good news of Jesus with other people. Sometimes we seem to imagine that telling other people about Jesus is a bit like advising them to go to the dentist and get their teeth fixed. It is hardly good news. We need to remind ourselves that the kingdom is a delight. On the basis of these passages, mission evangelism is really about inviting people to a party!

## 4. The kingdom is *divisive*

Although the kingdom is a delight, we are also reminded that there is something divisive about it. We learn in the gospels that not everybody enters the kingdom. There is to be a division of good fish and bad fish (Matthew 13:47–48), wheat and the chaff (Luke 3:17), wheat and weeds (Matthew 13:24–29), wise and foolish bridesmaids (Matthew 25:1–13), sensible and faithless stewards (Matthew 25:14–30) and sheep and goats (Matthew 25:31–46). Elsewhere, Jesus contrasts the kingdom of heaven with an alternative: hell (Mark 9:47).

The lesson here is the vital importance and the implications of the kingdom of God. Our destiny hinges on how we respond to Jesus' offer of the kingdom. To use another image found in the gospels, we either stand firm on the foundation stone of the kingdom or we trip to destruction over it (Luke 20:17–18). We can all remember the bitter disappointment we had at missing out on some party or festivity. How infinitely more terrible it will be for someone to realise that they have missed out on eternity's party!

## 5. The kingdom requires a *decision*

It is because of the value and the significance of the kingdom of God that action is required (Matthew 21:28–32; Luke 16:16). We are to be like a person selling all he has in order to buy the great pearl or the field with the buried treasure (Matthew 13:44–46). The kingdom must be seized speedily, joyfully and at any expense. It is not enough to sit idly by and hope that the kingdom will fall into our hands. It will not. We must take action, however costly and radical it may be. This is too good an offer to miss!

The lesson here is of the vital importance for us and for others of choosing the kingdom of God. Life is full of decisions, some of which we get wrong, but to choose the kingdom is the most important decision we can make and one that we must not get wrong. We must make the decision and we must do all we can to persuade others to make it.

## 6. The kingdom makes *demands*

The kingdom is entered by having a childlike faith and trust in Jesus. However, it doesn't stop with entry into the kingdom. We are repeatedly encouraged to live by the values of the kingdom. In Matthew 21:43 Jesus warned the entire nation of Israel that unless they produced proper fruit, the kingdom would be taken away from them. There are great privileges in being a citizen of the kingdom of heaven, but there are also great responsibilities.

There are relatively few references to 'the kingdom of God' in the letters of the New Testament. This is partly because it was not such a helpful image for non-Jews, and partly because it was a potentially dangerous term in the Roman world where Caesar was the only king. Yet in several places Paul talks of the kingdom when he is requesting his readers to live properly as Christians. For example:

- 'For the Kingdom of God is not a matter of what we eat or drink, but of living a life of goodness and peace and joy in the Holy Spirit' (Romans 14:17).
- 'For the Kingdom of God is not just fancy talk; it is living by God's power' (1 Corinthians 4:20).
- 'Don't you know that those who do wrong will have no share in the Kingdom of God?' (1 Corinthians 6:9).

The implication is plain. We are not just to get into the kingdom; we are to live lives that are appropriate to being in the kingdom. We need to live like the King's children.

## THE TIMETABLE OF THE KINGDOM

Some people ask, 'Is the kingdom something in the present, or is it in the future? Has it come, or is it coming?'

Actually the right answer seems to be 'both'. Jesus taught that the kingdom was both here now and on its way. It had already arrived and yet was something for whose coming we were still to pray.

This may sound like a contradiction but it isn't. Think of a couple who get engaged to each other. In getting engaged they start to enjoy some, but not all, of the benefits and responsibilities of being married. They spend more time together, share deeper confidences and are able to plan for a joint future. To

---

**God's kingdom is like being engaged.**

---

be engaged is an enjoyable situation; yet it would be very strange if the couple wanted their engagement to last for ever!

The whole point of an engagement is that it leads to the final state of marriage.

God's kingdom is like this. When we become followers of Jesus we enter the kingdom. It is a bit like being engaged in that although it is wonderful, there is something preliminary and temporary about it. It is only the first step. Equally, we look forward to the future, and as Christians we wait expectantly for the final and complete fulfilment of the kingdom when Jesus comes again.

So although they are linked, there is both a present and a future kingdom of God.

## The present kingdom of God

At the moment the kingdom of God is hidden and its full glory is obscured. The kingdom occurs wherever people's hearts, minds and lives have been surrendered to Jesus, and he has been made their King. Although the kingdom is not something we can see, we can see its fruits.

Imagine a husband and wife who say that they love each other deeply. But how can we see that invisible and mysterious 'love'? The answer is so obvious that we take it for granted: we see it in how they behave towards each other. We are happy to believe that they love each other when we see them, day after day, showing acts of kindness and forgiveness towards each other. We would be very sceptical about this love if their marriage were one long battle. So it is with the kingdom. We can know it is there because we see the evidence of it. Wherever followers of Jesus are working to bring hope to the hopeless, food to the hungry, love to the unloved, justice to those deprived of justice, there we find the kingdom of God.

I want to emphasise this because it is an area where some Christians have got themselves into difficulties in that they seem to feel that the kingdom is something so private and 'spiritual', it doesn't affect how they live.

Let me highlight three points.

### The kingdom is not just about the future, it is about the present

Some people seem to view the kingdom as really only having something to do with the future. They seem to think that when they die, or when Christ comes again, will be when belonging to the kingdom really matters. In the meantime it is a bit like a pension policy; they keep it safely locked away, waiting for the day when they will cash it in.

It is important that we do not think of the kingdom as only being in the future. Yes of course, in its fullest, most complete and most glorious sense, it will be in the future, but there is also a very important present-day aspect to the kingdom. We are called to live out kingdom values every day. Feeding poor people, befriending lonely men and women, visiting prisoners, working for a better, fairer, cleaner future for Jesus' sake is all part of what the kingdom is about.

Jesus expects us to pray on a daily basis that his kingdom will come, but he also expects us to work for it to come with the same frequency.

### The kingdom is not just about the spiritual, it is about the physical

Some Christians believe that the really important work is saving souls, because in their view this world is passing away. The result is that we end up with two worlds: the spiritual (invisible and important) and the physical (visible and trivial).

I fail to see this division in the Bible. You do not find it in the Old Testament, with all its cries for justice and mercy; you do not find it in the ministry of Jesus, who healed the sick, fed the hungry and preached about helping the poor; and you do not find it in the letters of the New Testament. Neither do you find it in the history of Christianity, where the church has given rise to a vast number of doctors and nurses, founders of schools, hospitals and orphanages and social reformers.

Some people suggest that this makes for hard decisions. Do we have evangelistic meetings or do we plant trees? Do we visit the sick or do we pray for their souls? Do we proclaim truth in pulpits or do we give soup to the homeless? The answer is straightforward. We do both, and if we can do them together so much the better. After all, as someone has said, a starving belly has no ears.

### The kingdom is not just for the church, it is for the world

Still others believe that the only real place where the kingdom is exhibited is inside church on Sunday or, just possibly, during midweek meetings as well. There, amid pews and hymns or seats and songs, is where the kingdom is proclaimed, and there is where, briefly, the kingdom is present. Linked with this is the view that ministers, vicars and pastors work for the kingdom full time, while the rest of us are merely able to be involved for a few brief hours a week.

By now you have probably guessed my response to this! I see this as unbiblical and unhelpful. The idea that the kingdom is confined to particular places must be one of the devil's smartest lies. We are to pray that God's will is done over the whole world ('as it is in heaven'), and God's will is that the whole world (which includes our homes, offices and even our sports clubs) is to come under his rule. There is nowhere from which the kingdom of God is to be excluded – no little patch over which the devil can claim unlimited sovereignty. If the kingdom is where Christ rules and God's will is done, then the battle line between God's kingdom and the devil's kingdom lies everywhere we go. At home or at work, we can aim to see the kingdom of God extended, or we can allow it to be pushed back by the forces of the evil one. Wherever we are, we must be a witness to the kingdom and we must work to bring the King's standards to bear on every area of our lives.

Someone has called this phase of God's kingdom 'the kingdom of grace'. By calling it that they are drawing attention to the vital fact that it is a kingdom with doors that are constantly open. You can still enter God's kingdom. It is the kingdom of grace, because it is in the present that God's special kindness (which is what 'grace' means) is extended to everybody.

It is this stage of the kingdom of God that we live in. It is hidden, yet made visible by the actions of the King's followers. However, the Bible teaches that one day, without warning, this will come to an end.

## The future kingdom of God

Consider again our engaged couple. They look forward with longing to their wedding day. That day will end their engagement and transform the relationship into a marriage. As it does so, everything the engagement stood for will be fulfilled.

Just as the wedding transforms their engagement, so one day will God's kingdom be transformed. At some time in the future, on a date unknown and without any warning, Christ himself will come back in glory and awesome power, and the whole world will see him as the glorious King of the universe. At this Second Coming, the kingdom of grace will instantly change into the kingdom of glory. What was hidden and only partially seen will become public and glorious, and what was provisional and temporary will be replaced by something that is complete and final. At a stroke, the hostile evil forces that are now battling against God will be overthrown. In a vision, Revelation 11:15 records what will be announced: 'The seventh angel sounded his trumpet, and there were loud voices in heaven, which said: "The kingdom of the world has become the kingdom of our Lord and of his Christ, and he will reign for ever and ever' (NIV).

On that day, earth's rebellion against heaven will finally be over, and the kingdom of God will be victorious. As Christ comes there will be one other solemn change to the kingdom: the opportunity of entering it will end. The door will be closed. When the kingdom comes visibly, then it will be too late for anyone to say to Jesus, 'I want to be in the kingdom!'

Some curious people have peered, Bible in hand, into the future to try and work out the date of Christ's coming. I can sympathise, since our attitude to quite a few things (like pension plans, mortgages and 20-year investments) would change if we knew that the world was ending in 2015. However, those who search so hard are wasting their time. In Matthew 24:36 Jesus specifically said about the time of his return, 'However, no one knows the day or the hour when these things will happen, not even the angels in heaven or the Son himself. Only the Father knows.'

We do not know when the coming will be. It may be today or tomorrow, but it might not be for centuries. Wise people will *plan* as if Christ's coming will not occur in their lifetime, but *live* as if it will occur tomorrow. That is the right balance.

Rather than encourage you to pursue speculation about dates and times, let me suggest that you focus on the two practical lessons of the Second Coming that are celebrated throughout the letters of the New Testament.

The first lesson is that Christ's return should be a great encouragement to us. However bleak our present circumstances (unemployment, age or disability), our future is glorious. For Christians, the best is yet to come. Our present experience of the kingdom is just a faint foretaste of the wonderful glory that awaits us in the future (Romans 5:2; Colossians 1:27; Titus 2:13). It is not only we who have been given hope and purpose by this truth; our world now has a purpose. History is not a blind random process; it is moving towards the coming of Christ in glory and with him the great eternal kingdom of glory.

The second lesson is that Christ's coming must not surprise us. When suddenly he acts to end history as we know it, it is vital that we are found to be those who are both praying and working for the kingdom to come. We are to stay alert and on duty (Mark 13:33, 35–37).

## Practical implications

### Think about how you pray

What does it mean to pray for the kingdom to come and God's will to be done?

It means several things. If, for a moment, we stay focused on the present kingdom, then we must realise that it means we want God's rule to be extended. To return to the image of the out-of-control orchestra or choir, we are praying here that more of the instruments and players start joining in with heaven's tune rather than their own.

Let's think about this individually. It's easy to think of our coming into the kingdom as a single, one-off, once-for-all event. We invite Jesus into our lives and that's that. Of course there is more. Conversion is just the beginning; we are not simply to be saved, we are to become like Christ. We need to pray this prayer, 'Your kingdom come, may your will be done', continually for our own lives. When we say to Jesus, 'Come into my life and be my Lord and King,' generally we do not realise quite how radical the changes are that he needs to make. If we imagine our lives as being houses, then conversion is opening the door to invite Jesus in to take charge. We can tend to hope that he will be contented merely to rearrange the furniture or straighten the pictures in the living room; we can live with that! The problem is, it soon emerges that Jesus wants to completely modify the whole house. He wants to fling open cupboards, throw things away, knock down walls and make any number of changes. To pray, 'Your kingdom come, may your will be done' means we are to open up everything that our lives are to Jesus' authority. 'Be Lord of everything' we should pray, and we should mean it. Are there areas of your life (your relationships, your work, your leisure activities, your career hopes, your money) where Jesus' influence is minimal? Praying this prayer (rather than just saying the words) means giving Jesus the freedom to take charge. What we are saying in asking for the kingdom to come and God's will to be done for our lives is that we want to be obedient to God's commands.

We should also think about other people when we pray this part of the Lord's Prayer. Of course, if people are not Christians, by praying this we are asking that they come to faith in Christ. This is certainly something we should pray for all those we work with or meet who are outside the kingdom of God entirely. If we pray for our Christian friends, we should ask that God's rule and dominion would extend throughout every area of their lives. We should particularly perhaps pray for those with whom we are in fellowship in our churches.

Praying for God's kingdom to come should not stop with our friends and ourselves. We need to pray for the kingdom to come in the world about us. We need also to pray that the values of our world would come to reflect, more and more, the values of God's kingdom. Those values include love, justice, truth and peace. We know that this world will never know any of these perfectly before Christ's Second Coming, but we are under orders to do what we can. Of course, in praying for the kingdom to come, we are also praying that the devil's kingdom, with the greed, envy, hate, violence, darkness and abuse that it spreads, will be defeated.

The short-sighted Christian fails to see beyond their immediate circle of friends and contacts so that what God is doing in the big wide world beyond is only a distant blur. Even though they may travel to Africa or Asia for business or holidays, they have little interest in the progress of the kingdom in these areas. The long-sighted Christian is more rare, but does exist. They are so busy peering into the distance that they fail to see what is happening around them. They might be passionately concerned about the extension of the kingdom in, for example, South America, but they have little concern for what happens among their family or colleagues, or in their own town. I suppose we are all tempted one way or another. The fact is, we need to have a balanced interest; we need to pray for and support the kingdom both locally and globally.

So far our praying has concentrated on the present aspect of God's kingdom. But what about the future? Well, in praying that the kingdom may come we are not simply to restrict our praying to the present kingdom of grace being extended through this world. Instead, we are to pray that the kingdom of glory may come as well. As the engaged couple long for their marriage, so we are to long for the public and permanent fulfilment of the kingdom. Or, as tortured and maltreated people in a conquered land await an army of liberation to save them, so we pray urgently, 'May your kingdom come soon.' For the kingdom to come fully would mean an end to everything that ruins our lives at present.

In the kingdom of glory there will be no illness, separation, loss, despair or hatred. If you think that is overstating the matter, read the first few verses of Revelation 21:

Then I saw a new heaven and a new earth, for the old heaven and the old earth had disappeared. And the sea was also gone. And I saw the holy city, the new Jerusalem, coming down from God out of heaven like a beautiful bride prepared for her husband. I heard a loud shout from the throne, saying, 'Look, the home of God is now among his people! He will live with them, and they will be his people. God himself will be with them. He will remove all of their sorrows, and there will be no more death or sorrow or crying or pain. For the old world and its evils are gone for ever.' (Revelation 21:1–4)

Don't get me wrong. I enjoy life now. I enjoy this world and there are lots of things I want to do here on earth. I think that most Christians have the same attitude. Yet we cannot be blind to the fact that there is suffering, pain and death wherever we look. And as we compare this wonderful but flawed world with the one God has promised us, we can only say from the bottom of our hearts, 'May your kingdom come and come soon!'

Have you realised how serious a thing it is to pray 'your kingdom come'? By praying this we are asking for our history to come to an end. We are pleading for God's power to come in such a way that this world becomes a holy and perfect place, where all evil is driven out. It is an awesome prayer. In fact, for those who have rejected Jesus the King it is a terrifying prayer. When the King comes in glory, they will be on the wrong side of his kingdom for ever. The door to the great banquet will be firmly and finally closed. This should give us an urgency in the sharing of our faith with others. Every time we pray this prayer for the kingdom to come, we ought to remind ourselves that we must do what we can to bring others into the kingdom while there is still time.

To pray that God's kingdom will come should lift our spirits and fill us with hope under even the most difficult circumstances. It reminds us that the future is certain; God's total victory over evil is assured. One day God's kingdom, now currently growing in secret, will suddenly blossom in glory.

However tragic this world's history may have been, the fact that the kingdom will come promises that its future will be wonderful beyond description.

## Think about how you live

Prayer and practice must work together. It is nowhere more true than here. It would be easy simply to pray for the kingdom to come and leave it to God, but that would be an abuse of prayer. God expects us to live out in our lives what we have prayed with our minds, hearts and mouths. He expects more from us than simply praying for the kingdom to come; he expects us to be those who also work to make the kingdom come.

This part of the Lord's Prayer sets out what should be the great priority of our lives. That priority is the extension of God's kingdom, and with it the honouring of his name and the carrying out of his will. We cannot pray this prayer with any

---

**It should be a truth that shapes our entire existence.**

---

sort of sincerity and then just go away and start building our own personal empires without any regard for his kingdom. His kingdom comes first.

The fact that we serve the kingdom should also be a truth that shapes our entire existence. As you watch the television or read a newspaper, remember you are a citizen of God's kingdom. What does God have to say on some of the matters you read about? Is there something you should pray about or something you should do? Think about where you live and take time to consider the area around you. God has put you in this place. What are you doing for the kingdom there? I could multiply such questions endlessly, but do you get the point? The kingdom is not just to be the priority of our prayers; it should be the priority of our lives too.

Now all this raises enormous issues. Let us consider just four of them.


## FOUR TOUGH ISSUES

### Issue 1: Seeking God's will for your life

'Ah yes,' says someone. 'I want to do God's will in my life. But how do I find God's will?' Many Christians get very troubled about this and I sympathise.

Let me make several points.

1.  We need to be constantly reminded that the issue is wanting to know God's will for us and not simply getting God to rubber stamp his approval on *our* will for ourselves. Prayer is not twisting God's arm; it is letting him direct our wills. It is his kingdom, not ours. That said, we have to be wary of thinking that God always wants us to do what we do not want to do. God gives us our gifts for a reason and his will for us may well be what we really desire to do.

2.  We can come to know God's will best in more or less the same way as we come to know anybody else's will: by spending time being with them. We come to know God by reading his word, the Bible, through which he shows us his desires, commands and concerns. As we spend time

with the Bible, allowing the Holy Spirit to speak to us through God's words, we come to know both God and his will better. We also come to know God and his will by praying to him. In our communication with God the Father, again helped by the Holy Spirit, we come to know God's will for our lives. God can also speak to us through the church and can often confirm his will through circumstances.

3.  There are very many areas of our lives that are neither right nor wrong and about which it is probably rather naïve to seek God's will. For example, there are most certainly more important things to pray about than whether to change to skimmed milk or which tie to wear.

4.  More importantly, there are many areas of our lives over which God is concerned but on which he has already spoken in his written word. For example, God's will over matters to do with stealing is perfectly plain to everyone who has read the Bible. We don't need to pray about it. Someone once asked Mark Twain about the difficult passages in the Bible and received the reply that it was not the passages that he did not understand that worried him; it was the ones that he did. This is a very similar situation. For most of us, most of the time, it is not *knowing* God's will that is the problem; it is *doing* it.

5.  This still leaves a small number of difficult cases; for example what job to take, where to live and who to marry. These can be agonising decisions and sometimes trying to discern God's voice clearly about them can be very frustrating. I believe that sometimes God wants us to work out solutions to our problems by using our common sense and by talking

things over with wise and trustworthy Christian friends. Think of it this way: a wise parent will not make all the decisions for their child. That is hardly the way to produce maturity. Instead they will encourage the child to learn how to make decisions themselves. Sometimes God does the same.

6. Have an unbreakable general principle that you will seek the kingdom of God and the kingdom's good in all you do. Jesus makes a wonderful promise in Luke 12:31: 'He will give you all you need from day to day if you make the Kingdom of God your primary concern.' We need to trust him in that.

## Issue 2: Staying pure in an impure world

If you have taken on board the truth that on this planet there are two warring kingdoms, then it is obviously wise to decide that the only way to truly serve God is to have nothing to do with the opposition. 'I will serve God only,' you say defiantly, 'and I will have nothing at all to do with the kingdoms of this world. I will separate myself from all that stands against him.'

The problem is that as soon as you switch on the television, read the newspaper, go shopping or go to work, things become complicated. You are immediately faced with dealing with ungodly states, power-grabbing multinational corporations and politicians who are against God's kingdom values. So how do we live for the kingdom of God in a hostile world?

Traditionally there have been two responses to this problem of how to keep spiritually pure in a corrupt world. One is to try and isolate yourself: unplug the television, cancel the papers and only deal with Christian butchers and bakers. The other is to try to change your society. In the seventeenth century many European Christians tried to escape the wicked world by fleeing to America to create spiritually pure colonies. As you may have noticed, it didn't work!

The only real solution is a hard one. We are to represent God's kingdom in the middle of a hostile world. We are to live and work in this world without losing God's kingdom values. It's not easy but it seems to be the only way. Some of these issues came up in my book *Ten: Living the Ten Commandments in the 21st Century* (Kingsway, 2000).

The early church faced a far more hostile world than most of us will ever have to. For all the achievements of Rome, Roman rule was not the easiest of systems to live your life under, especially if your loyalty belonged to any other king than Caesar. Jesus himself was faced with this conflict when he was asked whether it was right to pay taxes to Caesar (Matthew 22:15–22). Like most of the questions to Jesus recorded in the Bible, it was a heavily loaded one. If Jesus said 'no' he would come out against Rome, and if he said 'yes' he would be a traitor to Jewish nationalism. Jesus' answer – 'give to Caesar what belongs to him. But everything that belongs to God must be given to God' – gives the principle that has guided thoughtful Christians ever since.

What Jesus is saying here is that Caesar has some authority, but the ultimate authority belongs to God. The worldly powers have some legitimate authority – they have been given rights in particular areas and in those areas they can make demands. But beyond that everything is God's. In fact Jesus, when talking to Pilate at his trial, makes the point that the world's powers are in fact given by God (John 19:11). What does this mean practically?

It means that we can deal with other kingdoms as long as we remember that God's kingdom has the ultimate and final authority. In matters of right and wrong, truth and honesty, God's rules cannot be broken. In many situations where a Christian is involved in the world, sooner or later there will come the point where they have to say to their employer, 'I'm unable to compromise my beliefs and values and cannot therefore do what you are asking me to do.'

The wise Christian will try to avert such a confrontation before it actually happens. It is sensible to indicate to those in authority over us that there are limits to our loyalty. But tough decisions have to be made sometimes and many Christians have paid a very high price for taking a stand for the kingdom. But if we are to stay part of the kingdom, then we must hold on to God's standards.

## Issue 3: How and where do I serve the kingdom?

In the light of the previous two issues I ought to say something about one question every serious Christian asks themselves at some time or other: 'Should I be in full-time Christian service?' After all, that way you could serve God and his kingdom with every resource you have. There would be no distractions and you could give yourself entirely to the work of the kingdom.

Obviously I cannot lay down specific rules for particular cases, but I can suggest some principles.

1. Don't rule out full-time service for God in a secular non-Christian position. God may well want you to serve him in your present job or in a new job that has nothing to do with

Christian activities. After all, we can serve God's kingdom wherever we are. Obviously there are careers that are ruled out for Christians. I would, for example, have my doubts about anyone who said that they felt God had called them to be a mercenary soldier or to run a casino. But if we are praying for God's kingdom to come, then one answer to that prayer may be for more Christians to be called into TV advertising or Parliament.

2. Don't rule out full-time service in a Christian position. God may indeed want your talents in such an area. Seek his will for your life and do not close off any doors until he does.

3. Whatever you do, consider your job as serving God and try to bring him glory in it. That may be hard and it may require much thought and prayer. Working for the kingdom in the workplace is not a matter of saying grace before meals in the staff cafeteria and having a Bible verse hanging over your computer! It may be up to you to put some morality into your company's shaky ethics; it may fall to you to try and act as peacemaker between warring factions in the office. And you may get precious little thanks for doing it.

4. Don't get the idea that there is a ladder of Christian service. With this view (which is very common) there are ordinary Christians who, say, work for the Inland Revenue or who care for children. Then there are super-Christians who pastor churches and run Christian projects. Above them are the super-super-Christians who plant churches in Mongolia. The fact is that all Christians should work for the kingdom wherever they are. God alone knows who serves him longest and hardest and he will, in his time, reward them accordingly.

## Issue 4: I want to see the kingdom come but all I have is the church!

Before finishing this chapter I want to deal with one final difficulty. This centres on the fact that for many people the church can be, for at least some of the time, a rather disappointing experience. The problem is that people read their Bibles and come across these great truths about the kingdom of God and they say, '*Amen.* That's great. That's what I want to see: fellowship, selfless sharing, healings, great teaching, works of power, peace, joy, love and justice!' Then they go to church . . .

You may have a great church that seems as if it has just come out of the pages of the Bible. In which case praise God, enjoy it and skip the next few paragraphs. But other people's experience is different. They look around them and say, 'Is this really it?' There seems to be such a discrepancy between the kingdom and the church that they get disillusioned. Now if this is you, let me make some suggestions.

1. Remember that the church and the kingdom of God are separate things. The local church is the working out of the kingdom through sinful men and women like you and me. This is not simply a cliché; it is true. Imagine, for example, someone with a difficult personality who becomes a Christian. Now they *may* undergo a radical and overnight personality change as a result of their conversion, but it is far more likely that it is something God will deal with over many years. So in the meantime, they bring their personality problems to church. If you read the New Testament letters carefully you see that even within the first decades of

the history of the church there were problems. In Acts 6 we find out that there were disagreements between the Greek and Hebrew speakers. The Corinthian church seems to have had more than its fair share of problems. In the time between Paul writing his letter to the Ephesian church and John including his brief message to the Ephesians from the risen Christ in Revelation (2:1–7) things had slipped in Ephesus. Yet the kingdom is more than the church.

2. Be wary of having a fantasy Christianity. We live in a world in which all sorts of fantasies abound. For instance there is fantasy marriage, where X and Y fall in love, get married, have endless wonderful sex, never have arguments, produce beautiful children and somehow manage to stay healthy, wealthy and wise, living happily ever after. This is, of course, actually a cartoon version of the real thing. It is also a rather dangerous cartoon version because if we believe it we will inevitably find reality a disappointment. A similar sort of fantasy Christianity exists as well, and it tells us that the only real church is one where everything is perfect. There, wonderfully moving meetings occur in which beautiful people sing scintillating words over perfect music produced by talented musicians, and elegant, amusing and incredibly appropriate sermons of just the right length are delivered every Sunday without fail. And, of course, loving insightful Christian fellowship is on hand whenever you want it and never when you don't. Do you see the danger this poses? Disillusionment is guaranteed. As they say: get real!

3. Try to do what you can. In a church that is not really delivering, it is all too easy to start pointing the finger. It's far better to admit you fall below God's standard, to ignore

other people's failings and to say, 'Yes, we fall below God's standard. Is it my fault and is there anything I can do to improve matters?'

In a world where there is no purpose other than having fun, we desperately need to reassert the fact that our true purpose lies with God's kingdom and Jesus Christ the King. We are to serve the kingdom faithfully all day and every day; at home and at work; in our pleasures and in our struggles.

As we serve, we serve joyfully and expectantly because one day the King will come. And as Jesus returns in indescribable glory, he will bring with him the kingdom in all its fullness and majesty. Everything that we and Christians through the ages have worked for will at last be fulfilled and completed. This prayer will have been fully answered.

## QUESTIONS

- If your political party uses a manifesto in which it suggests that it will bring in a new and perfect era of justice and right-eousness in this country, do you say 'Amen' or accuse them of trying to do what only God can do?
- Should Christians be optimists or pessimists?
- What would it mean for God's kingdom to be extended in your workplace or your community? What practical steps can you take to help make it happen?
- Are you more concerned about the kingdom locally or globally? How can you be more balanced in your concerns?

# 5

# Provision

*Give us this day our daily bread.*
(Traditional)

*Give us our food for today.*
(New Living Translation)

## THE SECOND HALF OF THE LORD'S PRAYER: OUR NEEDS

We have now come to the second part of the Lord's Prayer and with it a shift in focus. The prayer is no longer centred on 'you' and 'your'; it is now centred on 'us' and 'our'. This shift matches Jesus' subdivision of the Law in Mark 12:29–31. There, one of the teachers of religious Law asked him,

> 'Of all the commandments, which is the most important?' Jesus replied, 'The most important commandment is this: "Hear, O Israel! The Lord our God is the one and only Lord. And you must love the Lord your God with all your heart, all your soul, all your mind, and all your strength." The second is equally important: "Love your neighbour as yourself." No other commandment is greater than these.'

115

Jesus' answer reflects the Ten Commandments, where the first five commandments are to do with our relationship to God and the second five are to do with our relationship to others.

Although this shift in focus can be exaggerated, it is important. This arrangement suggests Jesus' priority in prayer and I believe that we should model our priorities on his. The need for God's name to be glorified, God's kingdom to be extended and God's will to be done must all come first, and before our own needs. In an age in which being self-centred is normal, and indeed even praised as a virtue, we need reminding of this.

That said, there are dangers in over-emphasising this division. We might fall into the trap of thinking that having prayed for what God wants, it is now time for us to twist God's arm to give us what we want. The fact is that because we have become the Father's children, what he desires is what we should desire too. And equally because he is our Father he delights to give us what we truly need.

Praying the Lord's Prayer is an exercise in adjusting our desires to God's desires. If we think of the Lord's Prayer as a template for our lives, then what we need to do is adjust our lives according to it. Imagine someone installing a kitchen. They take the measurements and draw up the plans and then they cut everything to exactly match the shapes drawn on the design. The Lord's Prayer serves the same function as the plans: it lays out God's design for our lives and our task is to try and make our lives match that. So when we do pray for what we consider to be our needs, we must be aware that what we are praying for is for our lives to increasingly resemble God's master plan for them.

As we come to this part of the prayer, let us remember that we are not praying to God in order that he would give us what we want; we are praying to God in order that we might become the sort of people he wants.

With that in mind let us look at exactly what it is that Jesus is asking us to pray here.

## WHAT DOES IT MEAN TO ASK FOR OUR DAILY BREAD?

There has been much discussion over what, in this brief petition, Jesus really meant. The differences in interpretation are to some extent reflected in the two translations. The two main issues revolve around 'bread'/'food' and 'this day'/'for today'.

### 'Bread'

Bread was the staple food of the Bible lands. It was either eaten on its own or used as an edible wrapping around other food. It was also the most basic of foods. There were luxury items in the diets of people in Jesus' day (meat, honey, olive oil, grapes, figs, etc.), but this prayer does not include them. It stops with bread. In fact bread came to be almost synonymous with 'food'. If you didn't have bread, you starved. That's why the New Living Translation uses 'food' rather than 'bread'. That's fine as long as you remember that behind this word is the sense of a basic essential food to keep you alive rather than some five-course cordon bleu meal.

It is plain that 'bread' here is a figure of speech. Its meaning certainly extends to all food. It also extends beyond food to include everything we need for life. Christians have generally considered that under 'our daily bread' was included our physical needs (shelter, clothing, food, water, heating, health, money and medicine, to name just a few), our psychological needs (peace of mind, hope, encouragement) and our spiritual needs (strength from God, awareness of God's plan and purpose for us, etc.). It covers provision in the very widest sense of the word.

But there is even more to the meaning of 'bread' than this. As Jews, those listening to Jesus would have read far more into the word 'bread' than we do. The great central event in their history was the Exodus, where God had brought his people out of Egypt and taken them through 40 years of wandering in the wilderness into the Promised Land. During that time in the wilderness they had been kept alive by God, who had fed them with manna, a mysterious and miraculous food that took the place of bread.

The entire passage of Exodus 16:13–31 is very helpful here. To summarise the relevant points about manna:

- Manna was a fulfilment of the Lord's promise to Moses that he would give his people bread. Psalm 105:40 says, 'He gave them manna – bread from heaven.'
- Manna appeared on a daily basis in quantities that were adequate for that day and that day alone. It could not be stored, therefore it needed to be collected daily.
- The exceptions to this were the sixth day of the week when twice as much manna appeared, and the seventh day (the Sabbath) when nothing appeared. The manna that arrived on the sixth day could be stored for a day.
- This manna appeared without fail for 40 years, feeding the entire nation of Israel until the Promised Land was reached.

To Jesus' listeners these things that happened when God rescued his people from slavery in the Exodus were central to their faith. I could imagine that any Jew faced with a shortage of food would have turned to God and prayed something like, 'Lord, you miraculously provided my ancestors in the wilderness with bread, so please provide for me now.' The word 'bread' should remind us therefore that God has a superb track record of supplying his children with food, even under the most unpromising of circumstances. It might also have suggested to them that Jesus was the new Moses, who could lead the people in a new Exodus.

The word 'bread' would have pointed back to what God had done for his people in the past. It would also have pointed to the future. Among the prophecies associated with the coming Messiah was that he would have a great banquet. We read about this in Isaiah 25:6–10:

> In Jerusalem, the LORD Almighty will spread a wonderful feast for everyone around the world. It will be a delicious feast of good food, with clear, well-aged wine and choice beef. In that day he will remove the cloud of gloom, the shadow of death that hangs over the earth. He will swallow up death for ever! The Sovereign LORD will wipe away all tears. He will remove for ever all insults and mockery against his land and people. The LORD has spoken! In that day the people will proclaim, 'This is our God. We trusted in him, and he saved us. This is the LORD, in whom we trusted. Let us rejoice in the salvation he brings!' For the LORD's good hand will rest on Jerusalem.

Jesus himself used images of banquets and feasts when he talked of the coming of the kingdom in glory. In praying 'Lord, give us bread' Jesus' original hearers would probably have been looking forward expectantly to the great day of the coming kingdom when they would eat with him as King. This then would have overlapped with the prayer for the kingdom to come. Similarly, as followers of Jesus, we can look forward with eager expectation to the forthcoming celebrations when he comes again.

---

**Not 'pie in the sky when we die' but 'bread on the plate while we wait'.**

---

For many of Jesus' hearers then, and certainly for those since, the issue is not 'pie in the sky when we die' but 'bread on the plate while we wait'! This is frankly a very down-to-earth and practical prayer.

### 'Daily'

The second issue is what the word translated 'daily' or 'for today' means. It is a puzzling word, almost entirely unknown apart from this passage. What seems almost universally agreed is that the prayer is for our short-term and immediate needs. It is not 'grant us, Lord, such a vast quantity of food that we will never need to ask you again' but rather something like 'grant us enough food for this very day'. It concentrates on the immediate and looks no further than today. It looks for bread that, like the manna, God gives only on a daily basis.

So this part of the Lord's Prayer is very much a one-step-at-a-time prayer. But then faith is pretty much a one-step-at-a-time business.

## How God answers this prayer

This is probably a good point to talk about how we expect God to respond to a prayer for our needs. Some people talk a lot about miraculous answers to prayer; for example abrupt, remarkable healing that leaves the doctor baffled, a mysterious gift of money that arrives just when a financial crisis seems imminent or an amazing offer of accommodation that comes out of the blue. They happen. But so do the other sorts of answers to prayer. For example, for one person an illness gradually responds to antibiotics while another gets the strength to endure the illness. Equally, someone may get a job that allows them to earn enough to slowly pay off their debts and for another person the housing authority finds them a vacant flat. In fact the word 'miraculous' is a tricky one to define (getting the job, or the antibiotics taking effect, may be miraculous really). Some talk about 'spectacular' answers to prayer and that may be better. But please don't think that there are two categories of answers to prayer: First Class (spectacular) and Second Class (not-so-spectacular). Both are answers to prayer, and let's thank God for both.

I mention this because when we pray we should not limit how God is to work. In the wilderness God supplied Israel with bread in an amazingly spectacular way. For most of history, however, God has supplied bread through the much less head-line-grabbing way of farmers producing grain and bakers baking it and people having the money to buy it. And let's not forget that God provides the grain, waters it through rain and makes it grow.

The same rule applies where we pray for other needs, whatever they are. God may give a dramatic and spectacular answer to prayer or he may give an answer so subtle that it is hard to see his hand in it. Some Christians expect the spectacular and are disappointed at anything less. Other Christians only expect the ordinary, never the spectacular, and are astonished when it happens. Don't rule out either option. However God answers, praise him.

Now let us look at something that I feel is extremely important.

## THE PHYSICAL VERSUS THE SPIRITUAL?

There is a shift in focus occurring as we move from the first part of the Lord's Prayer into the second. Some people feel it is more drastic than that; they feel it is an abrupt and noisy grinding of gears. There we were praying about God's kingdom, about his name being glorified and his will being done and now suddenly we are asking God for bread of all things! Of course, in reality, we are not just praying about bread, but mortgage repayments, friends with illnesses, dry rot in the cellar and children with nappy rash.

Some people have felt that this change between the first and second part of the Lord's Prayer is so drastic that it is hard to accept. They have even gone so far as to try and alter the meaning of these words. They suggest that, of course, Jesus didn't mean *real* bread! He couldn't possibly have meant the stuff we buy from the supermarket and eat to fill our stomachs. No, they say, what he was really referring to was the Bible or the Lord's Supper in some way. It is far more 'spiritual' than real 'physical' bread.

This is one of Christianity's disastrous mistakes. Throughout the history of the Christian church there have been a number of truly bad ideas. Some of these are pretty obvious: authorising the dreadful slaughter of the Crusades, burning heretics and so on. Others have been less obvious but no less disastrous. One such mistake was dividing the world from heaven and the spiritual from the physical. With this view (which everybody blames on the Ancient Greeks!) there are two realms in the universe: heaven and the world. One is non-physical, spiritual and pure and the other is physical, unspiritual and dirty.

If you adopt this view (which, despite enormous efforts, has never really been erased from Christianity) there are several probable results.

First, you develop a two-tier Christianity. In the upper level are those who can deal with spiritual matters, such as vicars, pastors, priests and nuns. In the lower level is everybody else ('ordinary Christians', 'the man or woman in the pew') and they deal with the sinful and physical world. This leads very easily into the belief that those in the lower level can only talk to heaven by going through the upper level. Equally, very soon those in the lower level come to believe that prayer and talking to non-Christians about Jesus is the responsibility of the trained professionals of the upper level. This is a temptation that occurs right across many churches.

Second, you believe that the only things that matter are to do with heaven. The really important things in life are praying or worshipping in church. They are spiritual activities. Being a wife or a husband, an employer or an employee has nothing to do with spiritual matters because it is to do with this world. This spills over into how we view places: church or chapel, for example, is 'a holy place' while your workplace or home is not.

Expressed like this, do you see how disastrous this is? Everything gets put into compartments. Your Christianity need never really be used in your place of work or your family; it is too spiritual for that.

Third, to be involved with earthly matters is therefore second best. The best thing a Christian can do is to cultivate a completely 'spiritual' and other-worldly attitude. Spiritual things are all that matters. Because it is physical, this world is not really important at all.

Thankfully, the Holy Spirit (coupled with common sense) has frequently triumphed over this view. Christians have got involved in the world. There is a long and very honourable history of Christians building schools and hospitals, reforming unjust laws and improving society (for example, Shaftesbury, Wilberforce and Martin Luther King). At the time, though, those who did these things were made to feel rather odd by others who felt they were getting too involved in the non-spiritual world.

The root of the problem is that we have misunderstood what the word 'spiritual' means. We have assumed that the spiritual world is less real and less solid than the physical world around us. Endless works of religious art have made us think, for example, that in heaven, angels are so insubstantial that you can see through them and they can sit on clouds. The biblical picture of things is actually very different. Heaven is not less real than this earth; it is *more* real.

The apostle Paul in 1 Corinthians 15:44 talks about the resurrection body as being 'spiritual': 'They are natural human bodies now, but when they are raised, they will be spiritual bodies. For just as there are natural bodies, so also there are spiritual bodies.' So far the only risen human body we have an account of is that of Jesus. The resurrection accounts seem to go out of their way to point out that the risen 'spiritual' Jesus was not in any way less than pre-resurrection 'physical' Jesus. In Luke 24:36–43 Jesus specifically demonstrates that he is solid:

> . . . as they were telling about it, Jesus himself was suddenly standing there among them. He said, 'Peace be with you.' But the whole group was terribly frightened, thinking they were seeing a ghost! 'Why are you frightened?' he asked. 'Why do you doubt who I am? Look at my hands. Look at my feet. You can see that it's really me. Touch me and make sure that I am not a ghost, because ghosts don't have bodies, as you see that I do!' As he spoke, he held out his hands for them to see, and he showed them his feet. Still they stood there doubting, filled with joy and wonder. Then he asked them, 'Do you have anything here to eat?' They gave him a piece of broiled fish, and he ate it as they watched.

The other resurrection accounts mention how the disciples touched Jesus and ate with him. The fact that he was not limited by walls or locked doors may actually suggest that, far from being some sort of ghostlike apparition, the risen Jesus was more solid than the door or the wall.

The implications of this are profound. To be spiritual in the Bible's terms is not to be removed above the world, but rather to be in it. It is spiritual to be involved in this world's affairs. Real bread is just as spiritual as some imaginary and invisible 'heavenly bread'. I have no doubt that if we became more spiritual (again, in the Bible's meaning of the word) we would find ourselves more involved with the poor, the hungry and those discriminated against.

The Lord's Prayer brings heaven and earth together in a natural and rather unembarrassed manner. From asking that God's will be done, there is no hint that we are passing to something completely different as we go to asking for bread. Jesus expects us – and even encourages us – to pray for the needs of our bodies and those of others.

The New Testament letters follow Jesus' pattern and mark out no barrier between the spiritual and the physical. For example, chapters 1–11 of the letter to the Romans are full of the most mind-blowing theology and wisdom, and then in chapter 12 verse 1 Paul says, 'And so, dear brothers and sisters, I plead with you to give your bodies to God. Let them be a living and holy sacrifice – the kind he will accept. When you think of what he has done for you, is this too much to ask?' Over the next two chapters Paul provides the most practical and down-to-earth teaching on how to live. But the point is, it flows out naturally from what we might think of as the 'more spiritual' previous chapters. Paul knew no division between being spiritual and living smack bang in the middle of the problems of the world. Neither should we.


## PRACTICAL IMPLICATIONS

In previous chapters I have divided the practical implications into how we should pray and how we should live. Here any separation between what we should pray and how we should live is impossible. After all, how we live depends on how we pray. Yet as long as we realise that the division is artificial it may help us to continue to use the pattern we have used earlier.

## Think about how you pray

What does it mean to pray 'Give us our food for today'? Let me suggest three things.

### We are to be dependent

We live in a society that for most of the time is complacent, arrogant and sees itself as being totally independent of God. We imagine that life revolves around us, that as human beings we have mastered the world and that, with the aid of our technology, we can now do anything and everything. We are taught that we have rights and we are brought up to expect that we have an automatic right to treasure, leisure and pleasure.

This part of the Lord's Prayer speaks to that arrogance and over-confidence in our Western culture. We must ask God for even the most basic of our needs, our food. Just because our agriculture is enormously more sophisticated than in Jesus' time does not alter the fact that we still depend totally on God for what we eat.

We must remember that our ability to eat may be lost or we may not have anything to eat. Both appetite and food come from God. The same goes for all our other physical needs. When we consider how frail our flesh and blood is and how easily our lives can be ended, our declarations of independence from God seem the height of arrogance. Indeed it is a sobering thought that not a single person in this world can guarantee that they will still be alive in a week's time.

We must realise our dependence on God. The apostle James says: '. . . my dear brothers and sisters. Whatever is good and perfect comes to us from God above, who created all heaven's lights. Unlike them, he never changes or casts shifting shadows' (James 1:17). In 1 Corinthians 4:7 the apostle Paul asks: 'What makes you better than anyone else? What do you have that God hasn't given you? And if all you have is from God, why boast as though you have accomplished something on your own?'

'What do we have that God hasn't given us?' is one of those questions that should puncture any arrogance. Think of anybody who is any sort of success. What has made them what they are? Whether it is their intelligence, looks, speaking skills, business know-how or even inherited money, it is still something given by God. In fact, the English language acknowledges that, by talking about fortunate people as being 'gifted'. Our birth reminds us of the fact that everything we have in life is because it has been given to us by God; we arrive bearing nothing in our hands. Similarly when we die, we leave with nothing.

In the Old Testament, material prosperity is celebrated as a gift of God and even as a sign of God's blessing (see, for example, Deuteronomy 28:1–14; Job 42:12). Yet God, through Moses, warned the Israelites that one of the perils of prosperity and plenty was that it could make them independent of God. It is a message we need to take to heart in our proud and wealthy culture.

Beware that in your plenty you do not forget the LORD your God and disobey his commands, regulations, and laws. For when you have become full and prosperous and have built fine homes to live in, and when your flocks and herds have become very large and your silver and gold have multiplied along with everything else, that is the time to be careful. Do not become proud at that time and forget the LORD your God, who rescued you from slavery in the land of Egypt. Do not forget that he led you through the great and terrifying wilderness with poisonous snakes and scorpions, where it was so hot and dry. He gave you water from the rock! He fed you with manna in the wilderness, a food unknown to your ancestors. He did this to humble you and test you for your own good. He did it so you would never think that it was your own strength and energy that made you wealthy. Always remember that it is the LORD your God who gives you power to become rich, and he does it to fulfil the covenant he made with your ancestors. (Deuteronomy 8:11–18)

We need always to remember that everything we have comes from God himself. One reason why God limits the scope of this part of the Lord's Prayer to 'today' or 'tomorrow', is that it forces us to come to him day after day to ask for his assistance to give us food and all our other needs. We need to be dependent on God; it is the only safe position for us to be in.

## We are to be trusting

However, if our society is over-confident ('No sweat; we have the technology and we can do anything'), it also suffers frequent swings into near panic ('Help! The planet's in a mess; we're all going to die'). We are like that as individuals. One day we are assured, unworried, even complacent; we have money in the bank and the world is at our feet. The next day we are mortal, feeble and vulnerable and we wonder how we are going to survive.

This part of the Lord's Prayer doesn't just address our over-confidence; it also addresses our fears. You may not be able to put your mind at rest, but God can. The Bible is full of statements about how God provides. One of God's names in the Old Testament was *Yahweh yir'eh*, 'The LORD Will Provide' (Genesis 22:14).

Matthew records Jesus' teaching on wealth, possessions and security just after the Lord's Prayer at the end of chapter 6. These verses are really Jesus' comment on this part of the prayer.

'So I tell you, don't worry about everyday life – whether you have enough food, drink, and clothes. Doesn't life consist of more than food and clothing? Look at the birds. They don't need to plant or harvest or put food in barns, for your heavenly Father feeds them. And you are far more valuable to him than they are. Can all your worries add a single moment to your life? Of course not.

'And why worry about your clothes? Look at the lilies and how they grow. They don't work or make their clothing, yet Solomon in all his glory was not dressed as beautifully as they are. And if God cares so wonderfully for flowers that are here today and gone tomorrow, won't he more surely care for you? You have so little faith!

'So don't worry about having enough food or drink or clothing. Why be like the pagans who are so deeply concerned about these things? Your heavenly Father already knows all your needs, and he will give you all you need from day to day if you live for him and make the Kingdom of God your primary concern.

'So don't worry about tomorrow, for tomorrow will bring its own worries. Today's trouble is enough for today.' (Matthew 6:25–34)

Did you notice again the theme of being fed on a day-by-day basis? We would love to be given so much that we could just sit back complacently with the future assured, but that would be bad for us. God wants us to stay close to him. As part of that relationship he encourages us to trust him on a daily basis.

This is also a wonderfully liberating piece of wisdom. Have you noticed that so many of the things we worry about never actually occur? If you look far enough ahead you will find no shortage of things to worry about. As Corrie Ten Boom said, 'Worry does not empty tomorrow of its sorrow; it empties today of its strength.'

Of course, as expecting God to provide our daily bread doesn't mean that we sit back idly, neither does not worrying about the future mean that we cancel our pension. We are to plan for the future but we are to live day by day in faith.

### We are to be grateful

Gratitude is the response to answered prayer. In fact gratitude to God should be as regular as our heartbeat. We cannot pray for today's or tomorrow's bread without giving thanks for yesterday's!

Gratitude is a necessary action. As we realise that we are dependent on God, we ought to realise that the fact that we have travelled so far in our lives is due to God's mercy and goodness to us. Through its extraordinary advertising power, the world about us emphasises that there is so much we ought to want. And because of this it is good to remind ourselves that we have been so extraordinarily blessed by God. We have much to be thankful for.

In this context I recommend the practice of grace at meal times. Of course it can become a meaningless ritual (what can't?), and of course it is sometimes embarrassing in public places. But by publicly saying 'thank you' to God for each meal, we are reminding ourselves that it comes from him. We are also reminding ourselves that he has answered (and frequently more than answered) our prayer for 'daily bread'. And of course gratitude should not stop at food. When God supplies all our needs it is good and right to find time to thank him for his goodness to us. When was the last time you thanked God for all that you have been blessed with – your family, friends, home, possessions?

The prime motive for gratitude should be to honour God. However, it is also good for us because it helps fix in our minds what God has done for us. By thanking God we are making a thoughtful note that he has helped us so far. It is a reminder of God's faithfulness to us. Just as the Israelites looked back to the Exodus and reminded themselves that the Lord who provided for them then was still the same, so we should have things in our lives that serve a similar function. If we do, when we face difficult times we will be more able to say, 'God provided for me in the past, so I believe he can provide for me in the future.' As an aid to this, some people keep a prayer diary in which they write down situations where they have found that God has either answered prayer or has been especially good to them.

The apostle Paul, writing in Philippians 4:6–7, strikes what seems to be the right note of prayer and thanksgiving: 'Don't worry about anything; instead, pray about everything. Tell God what you need, and thank him for all he has done. If you do this, you will experience God's peace, which is far more wonderful than the human mind can understand. His peace will guard your hearts and minds as you live in Christ Jesus.'

Notice the phrase 'Tell God what you need, and thank him for all he has done'. Even this second part of the Lord's Prayer – when we consider our own needs – is not just to be making one request after another. It is to be giving thanks as well.

## Think about how you live

I suggest three guidelines here. But let me warn you in advance that far from being the least, the last of the three is actually the most challenging of them all.

### We are to live prayerfully

Far too often we treat prayer as merely the lubricant to our lives – when we come to a sticky spot we pour a bit on. The fact is, the Bible teaches that far from prayer being a little oil to make things run smoothly, we are to let it shape our lives. As we pray this part of the Lord's Prayer and think about what it means, we should deepen both our sense of dependence on God and our trust in him. We ought to look back with gratitude and look forward with expectation and hope.

We are to plan for the future but not be obsessed and preoccupied by it. We are to live day by day, rejoicing in God's goodness to us. We should live as if every day were our last, but we should plan as if we will live for many years.

### We are to live moderately

This prayer is for bread. It is for the very basics of life. As has been wisely said, it is a prayer for our needs and not our greeds. It is so easy to confuse what we want with what we really need. In fact, you could argue that the main purpose of modern advertising is to make us think that what we merely want is actually what we really need.

This prayer, and the Bible generally, gives us a very different perspective. Consider what the apostle Paul writes to Timothy:

> True religion with contentment is great wealth. After all, we didn't bring anything with us when we came into the world, and we certainly cannot carry anything with us when we die. So if we have enough food and clothing, let us be content. But people who long to be rich fall into temptation and are trapped by many foolish and harmful desires that plunge them into ruin and destruction. For the love of money is at the root of all kinds of evil. And some people, craving money, have wandered from the faith and pierced themselves with many sorrows. (1 Timothy 6:6–10)

According to Paul, moderation (just 'food and clothing') is good.

It is so important for us to let this part of the Lord's Prayer soak through into our lives. All day every day, society is shouting to us to 'desire more, get more and get it *now*'. Almost every week we seem to get letters from banks offering us yet more credit to buy more things. Not only do we need to resist these temptations to be greedy, we may need to oppose them positively. Perhaps in our praying we need to think about how we can live with less. In our prayers we need to come to God and ask him to show us how we can learn to live at the level he wants us to live. After all, we are far more likely to find contentment in seeking moderation than we are in desiring more.

Agur's prayer in Proverbs 30:7–9 is a wise one for us to make our own:

O God, I beg two favours from you before I die. First, help me never to tell a lie. Second, give me neither poverty nor riches! Give me just enough to satisfy my needs. For if I grow rich, I may deny you and say, 'Who is the LORD?' And if I am too poor, I may steal and thus insult God's holy name.

The Lord's Prayer gives a mandate to ask for necessities but no mandate to ask for luxuries. God may give us luxury and great wealth, but if God gives them to us we are to use them wisely.

## We are to live generously

This is the hardest of these three suggestions.

There are basically two groups of people in today's world. There are those who, when they say 'What shall we eat?', are expressing their difficulty in choosing because they have so much. Then there are those who, when they say 'What shall we eat?', are expressing their despair because they have nothing. What does this prayer, 'Give us our food for today', have to say to this?

Let us first consider a tough but related question: What about those people who pray this prayer yet still starve? Have they failed? To say that such people starve because they 'do not pray in faith' is to add insult to injury. Is the faith of those who prosper so superior? I think this is to misunderstand prayer. It is to imagine it as a tool with which we manipulate God, not as a means by which we try to make our lives into the pattern God wants.

Any theoretical or philosophical response to the problem of starving, as with the wider problem of suffering, must take in the whole issue of sin and evil in the world. Theologically, the world has been corrupted by evil and has fallen under the power of the evil one from whom Christ is gaining back control through the advancement of the kingdom. But that is only the theoretical or philosophical answer. I would hope that as any Christian stared at a starving person (whether Christian or not) on their television set they would not be content with it as a completely adequate response. The real response to such suffering is to do something about it and discuss its origin later. Jesus commanded us to do battle against evil, not to construct theories of its origin. Thankfully, that is what many Christians have done over the centuries.

This brings us back to the Lord's Prayer because we are reminded here, as elsewhere, that this prayer talks about 'our' and 'us', not 'mine' and 'me'. It is not a 'give me' prayer; it is a 'give us' prayer. When we pray for our needs we should also pray for the needs of others. And, of course, we need to do more than simply pray.

We have already seen that to be spiritual is not to be less concerned about the physical world; it is to be more concerned about it. It is precisely in this sort of area that only a true and real Christian faith will work. And in case I am accused of watering down the gospel, may I quote in my defence James, the brother of Jesus?

Dear brothers and sisters, what's the use of saying you have faith if you don't prove it by your actions? That kind of faith can't save anyone. Suppose you see a brother or sister who needs food or clothing, and you say, 'Well, goodbye and God bless you; stay warm and eat well' – but then you don't give that person any food or clothing. What good does that do?

> So you see, it isn't enough just to have faith. Faith that doesn't
> show itself by good deeds is no faith at all – it is dead and useless.
> (James 2:14–17)

Jesus ate with the poor and needy and brought into fellowship
with himself those who were on the margins of society. Perhaps
that is something we ought to take more seriously.

So when we pray, we also need to act. When, for example,
we ask God to solve the financial needs of one of our brothers
and sisters, we need to ask ourselves the question, 'Am I supposed to be the answer to this prayer?'

Our actions should be generous because God is and always
has been generous to us. Do we have more than we need? If
so, the automatic extension of this part of the Lord's Prayer
would be something like, 'Lord, thank you. You have given me
far more "bread" than I can use. Help me to use the surplus
wisely. Help me to be a responsible steward.' We often worry
about the fact that we do not have enough in our bank account.
Perhaps we ought to worry more about whether we have too
much.

We need to remember that we are not just individuals; we are
linked to those who are also followers of Jesus Christ with a
bond that is far stronger than even that of family ties. We and
they share the same Holy Spirit.

I would not be surprised if you found some of the questions
raised here about living moderately and living generously,
awkward and troubling. I do. If so, be encouraged. I do not
believe that God intended this prayer simply to be a tremendous comfort to us. He intended it to be the pattern around
which we should build our lives. I believe that in the area of

what we desire and how we give, most of us have deviated a very long way from God's pattern. As we pray this prayer and apply it, we may find that through it God is pushing our lives back into the shape he wants them to be. And that may be uncomfortable.

Yet it may also be amazingly rewarding, as we can never outgive God.

## QUESTIONS

- What sort of things do you think fall into the category of 'bread' in terms of our lives?
- Do we really believe that God is the provider of all we have?
- Why do we have to pray for bread on a daily basis? Can't we be trusted enough to ask for it once a week?
- Why do we prefer to have spectacular or 'miraculous' answers to prayer?
- What are the spiritual perils of poverty? What are the spiritual perils of prosperity? How do we guard against them?
- How do we strike a balance between having concern about the future and taking wise precautions?
- How can we live more generously in practical ways?

# 6
# Pardon

*And forgive us our trespasses,*
*as we forgive those that trespass against us.*
(Traditional)

*And forgive us our sins, just as we have forgiven those who have*
*sinned against us.*
(New Living Translation)

In some ways, this is the most difficult clause of the Lord's Prayer. It covers two interlinked issues: God's forgiveness of us and our forgiveness of other people. Both of these are major issues on their own. Forgiveness is not a subject that lends itself to cool, detached, theoretical discussion. Almost anybody who has talked publicly about the necessity of forgiving those who have hurt you will have had some sort of experience like someone coming up to them at the end of a meeting with a pale, angry face, blurting out, 'It's all right for you to talk about forgiveness, but let me tell you what happened to *me* . . .' Then, of course, they recount some absolutely appalling story of suffering, injustice and tragedy. Afterwards, the speaker wonders whether, if it had happened to them, they could have indeed forgiven . . .

Forgiveness is a serious matter. The best way to deal with it is by looking in turn at the two dimensions of forgiveness mentioned here: God's forgiveness of us and our forgiveness of others. These are not separate aspects of forgiveness. Far from it; they are very strongly linked. In fact throughout the New Testament the pattern is that it is because God has forgiven us that we are to forgive others. To go to the hard issue of human forgiveness without first understanding God's forgiveness of us in Christ would be illogical.

## GOD'S FORGIVENESS OF US

All the translations of the Lord's Prayer agree that we need to ask to be forgiven or pardoned by God as we, in turn, forgive or pardon others. Two questions arise immediately. First, what does it mean to be forgiven? Second, is our forgiveness of others the cause or the effect of God forgiving us? Let me deal with these questions in turn.

### What does it mean to be forgiven by God?

In order to understand God's forgiveness we need to understand what we are asking to be forgiven for. Here things are complicated by the fact that different forms of the Lord's Prayer use different words. In Matthew's version what we are forgiven can be literally translated as 'debts', while in Luke's version it is our 'sins'. Other versions used in churches talk about 'trespasses', 'transgressions' or 'offences' being forgiven. What do these words mean and which is the right one?

The shortest, simplest and most accurate translation is probably 'sins'. It is sins, not overdue financial loans, that Matthew's 'debts' refers to. However, don't entirely throw away the idea of pounds or dollars.

These various alternative words for 'sin' help fill out something of why we need forgiveness. In the New Testament the main idea behind the term 'to sin' is 'to miss the target' or 'to fall short'. The sense of the other words expands on this: to have *debts* is to owe someone something you cannot pay; to *trespass* is to be somewhere you should not have gone; to *transgress* is to cross a boundary that you shouldn't have; to *offend* is to injure or hurt someone. All these images, along with others, are used to describe the standing of human beings before God, and together these words produce a dark picture. We have fallen short of the target God has set; we have incurred debts to him that we cannot pay; we have strayed into places where we should not be; we have broken the boundaries he has defined; we have offended God's gentle, caring and loving nature towards us. The result is that the human race is in a hopelessly serious situation before God.

The Bible does more than give us a series of terms for sin; it also gives us the background to human sin – a casebook of examples, as well as a full diagnosis of the sinful condition.

The first few chapters of the book of Genesis outline the origin and spread of human sin. We read how the first man and woman were created with open access to God and were placed in the idyllic Garden of Eden where they had almost total freedom. Tempted by a mysterious creature, they chose to rebel against God and to break the one restriction he had placed on their freedom. The result was expulsion from the garden, separation from God, shame, punishment and eventually death. As a consequence, sin became part of the human nature and within a generation there was murder. Within a few more generations we read the following verdict in Genesis 6: 'Now the LORD observed the extent of the people's wickedness, and he saw that all their thoughts were consistently and totally evil . . . Now the earth had become corrupt in God's sight, and it was filled with violence. God observed all this corruption in the world, and he saw violence and depravity everywhere' (Genesis 6:5, 11–12). The rest of the Old Testament recounts how, despite God giving rules and commandments to his people, this pattern of deep-rooted sin persisted in the human race. The writer of the book of Ecclesiastes summed up the state of humanity: 'I discovered that God created people to be upright, but they have each turned to follow their own downward path' (Ecclesiastes 7:29).

Within the pages of the Bible we see examples of every kind of sin, almost as if to show us how widespread and varied it is. There are the sins that are denounced by our modern news-papers, such as greed, lust, adultery, murder; and all are con-demned. Yet the Bible also gives examples of more subtle and private sins: envy, betrayal, dishonour, hypocrisy, self-interest, arrogance, cowardice, secret malice, deception and the worship of people, possessions and activities. Despite the distance of time and culture that separates the world of the Bible from our own, all too often in the actions and words of the men and women recorded in its pages we catch an unflattering glimpse of ourselves. We are no different; we suffer from the same symptoms. Yet the Bible is not simply a list of various deeds. We see in its accounts the terrible deceptiveness of sin; the way sin promises but never delivers; the way sin offers to satisfy our needs but only aggravates them; the way sin holds out to us abundant life but only ever gives a creeping death. We also glimpse something of what all sin is ultimately about. It is the desire to be self-centred, to live as if we were God. It is to take his crown and put it on our head.

The Bible's diagnosis is that we are more than simply 'guilty' of sin, as if sin were just a simple criminal offence. It sees sin as a terrible deep-rooted infection that has worked its way into every aspect of being human. Sin has enslaved us (Romans 7:14, 23), pushed our lives off course (Isaiah 53:6) and made us unclean (Psalm 51:1–2). Sin has deceived us and corrupted us and, if untreated, will eternally destroy us. As the apostle Paul says in Romans 6:23, 'the wages of sin is death'.

Thankfully, for all its highlighting of this disease, the Bible also points out the cure: God's forgiveness. Only God's forgiveness is able to remedy all the many effects of sin.

When we think of that forgiveness and what it means, it is helpful to understand that there are two sides to forgiveness. One side of forgiveness involves the removal of sin, the other involves the restoration of our relationship with God. Although they are, or at least should be, linked, it is worth looking at them in turn.

*Forgiveness as the removal of sin*

Ultimately sin needs removing because it is a barrier that lies between God and us. Sin is a wall that must be broken down in order for us to relate to him properly. The idea of the removal of our wrongdoings lies behind so much of the language in the Bible about sin being 'taken away', 'covered' or 'washed away'. The parallel set of word pictures that we saw in Matthew's version of the Lord's Prayer talks about sin as an outstanding debt that has to be removed by being paid off or cancelled. Both sets of images are used in the Old Testament to explain how the sacrificial system worked and they are both used in the New Testament to explain the significance of the death of Jesus Christ.

---

## It is God, not us, who pays the debts or removes the sin.

---

God's forgiveness involves him taking away, or covering over, our sin. This forgiveness is always something that is done freely; it is God, not us, who pays the debts or removes the sin. This is what underlies the wonderful word 'grace'. Grace is the idea of God freely giving more than we dare to ask for; of God pouring out his favour on those who do not deserve it. We cannot earn forgiveness. After all, if someone could pay for what they had done wrong, it would not actually be forgiveness. A gas company does not say that you are forgiven when you pay your gas bill. You have paid it off yourself and that does not involve forgiveness. Forgiveness is always a generous act. In forgiving us, God has dealt with our falling short of the target, paid our unpayable debts, let us off our trespasses and transgressions and pardoned our offences. He has removed the sin barrier that lay between him and us.

Most people today do not consider sin at all; they have no concept of what it is, they do not realise that it is offensive to God and they do not consider that they personally are guilty of it. Even if they do think of it, they consider it to be a minor and private matter. Because sin is so trivial to them they think that it must also be trivial to God; his forgiveness is something that must surely be easily given. When he was dying, the nine-teenth-century German poet Heinrich Heine said, 'God will pardon me, it is His trade.' Many people today have a similar attitude. They presume that God can forgive just as easily as some billionaire could overlook an unpaid debt of five pounds. This overlooks the fact that our sinfulness is a very serious con-dition because rebellion against a perfect God is a far from trivial matter. For us to be forgiven our sins someone must pay for them and the Bible reveals that it is God himself who has paid the bill. The price of our forgiveness was that in Jesus, God himself suffered death on the cross. The apostle Paul summarises this exchange in terms of an unforgettable equa-tion: 'For God made Christ, who never sinned, to be the offer-ing for our sin, so that we could be made right with God through Christ' (2 Corinthians 5:21). Only God letting himself undergo the appalling agony of the crucifixion was able to win our forgiveness.

One of the most striking and moving passages in the whole Bible on what Christ did on the cross is to be found, not in the New Testament, but in the Old. Written around 700 years before the crucifixion, the whole chapter of Isaiah 53 is a prophecy about the fate of the coming Servant of the Lord, who although innocent himself, takes on the sin of his people and suffers in their place. Let me list some of the phrases used to describe what happens to the Servant. He is 'despised and rejected', 'acquainted with bitterest grief', 'wounded', 'crushed', 'beaten', 'whipped', 'oppressed', 'treated harshly', 'led as a lamb to the slaughter', 'led away to his death' and 'buried like a criminal'. At least seven times in a dozen verses it is made plain that these terrible sufferings are borne for others

– something summarised in this verse: 'He was counted among those who were sinners. He bore the sins of many and interceded for sinners' (Isaiah 53:12).

According to the Bible the barrier that our sin put up between us and God was so great and so serious that it could only be removed by the death of God's own Son.

## Forgiveness as the restoration of a relationship

In addition to talking about forgiveness as the removal of sin, the Bible also uses another set of images. Here the word pictures of forgiveness centre on the restoration of a relationship. The problem of the relationship between humanity and God is seen not so much in terms of a price to be paid or a debt to be cancelled, but rather as a broken relationship that needs repairing. The human race's rebellion against God has separated us from him; our once close and perfect relationship has been broken. God, however, desperately wants to bring us back into a right relationship with himself. His love drives him, so that people can be reconciled to him. This is the ultimate goal of his forgiveness – a complete reconciliation to the point that the breach in our relationship is completely healed.

This imagery of relationships is seen in the Old Testament in the way God talks about his bond with his people as that of a loving father with a child (Deuteronomy 1:31) or even as a spouse with an adulterous partner (as in Hosea). In the New Testament it is found in many places, particularly in the story of the Lost Son (Luke 15:11–32), as well as in all the language of God as 'Father' (e.g. 1 Corinthians 8:6; Ephesians 4:6). Perhaps the strongest images of the restoration of the relationship are found in the final chapters of the Bible. There, in

Revelation 21 and 22, we see how in the new heaven and the new earth, God now lives amid his people; the relationship that was broken in the Garden of Eden has now been restored.

In terms of relationships God's forgiveness means that although we were once guilty sinners, we are now God's children; although we were once enemies of God, we are now the friends of Jesus.

These two sets of images – sins removed and a relationship restored – are complementary and not contradictory. If God's love had not desired that the relationship with us be restored, Christ would never have gone to the cross. If Christ had not paid for our sin and so removed it, then God would never have been able to restore the relationship.

God's forgiveness is about the justice of removing the barrier of sin between him and human beings and about the love that wants to see that relationship restored. In Jesus Christ, and supremely in Jesus' death on the cross, love and justice meet.

## Which comes first – our forgiveness or God's?

There are two ways of reading this part of the Lord's Prayer, 'And forgive us our sins, just as we have forgiven those who have sinned against us'. One way to interpret this is to believe that our forgiveness of others is the cause of God forgiving us. The other way is to believe that we are to forgive in the same way and to the same extent as we ourselves have been forgiven. The question is therefore: Is our forgiveness of others the cause or the effect of God's forgiveness of us?

Since these views affect not only how we live but also our faith in Christ, I want to look at them carefully. The idea that our forgiveness comes first, suggests that when he comes to judge us, God looks at our record, notes that we were the forgiving sort and then lets us off accordingly. We would have earned our forgiveness by forgiving others. In fact any such belief is contradicted by the entire teaching of the Bible, which plainly states that it is God who has taken the initiative and forgiven us first. Of many possible verses let me mention just two here. In Colossians 2:13 the apostle Paul links God's forgiveness of 'all our sins' with Christ: 'You were dead because of your sins and because your sinful nature was not yet cut away. Then God made you alive with Christ. He forgave all our sins.' Ephesians 4:32 is one of a number of verses where we are commanded to do things because we have been forgiven through Christ: 'Instead, be kind to each other, tender-hearted, forgiving one another, just as God through Christ has forgiven you.' God's forgiveness comes first.

In fact the idea that the story of Jesus is 'good news' (which is what the word 'gospel' means) depends entirely on God forgiving us first. If whether or not we get forgiven by God rests entirely on whether we have forgiven others, then that is hardly particularly good news; it is at best a sort of conditional offer. This cannot be the case. All the New Testament language of praise about God's grace, love and peace only makes sense if God has freely, richly and amazingly forgiven us. Equally, the expressions of joy, celebration and certain hope that are found on almost every page of the letters of the New Testament can only arise from a forgiveness that has already been given.

This order ('I forgive you; now you go and forgive others') actually makes sound psychological sense. To be promised forgiveness conditionally ('I'll forgive you only if you forgive others') is guaranteed to result in tension, fear and uncertainty.

What, we ask, is the forgiveness 'pass mark'? Exactly how much forgiveness do we have to show? In contrast, to receive forgiveness is liberating. The price is already paid and we know we are forgiven. The result is joy, peace, certainty and gratitude.

There is one other question that must be addressed here. If Christians are forgiven when they come to faith in Jesus, then why do they continue to pray 'forgive us our sins'? The simplest answer is that when we become a Christian we are forgiven our sins in Jesus Christ, made a child of God and given his Holy Spirit to live in us. Nevertheless, on a day-by-day basis we still do things that come between us and our relationship with God, and we need to come to God daily to confess them. Failure to do so would be to damage our relationship with our heavenly Father – something that no child of God would want to happen. We have not just been brought back into a loving relationship with our Father, we want to keep that relationship unstained by even the slightest rebellion. For the Christian, unforgiven sins are like clouds in the spiritual sky; they soon accumulate to cut out the light. If we fail to keep a clean slate with our heavenly Father we will find that we will soon lose the joy and peace that are the privilege of every child of God.

## OUR FORGIVENESS OF OTHERS

The first dimension of forgiveness is God's forgiveness of us. The second dimension is our forgiveness of others. As we saw earlier these two are linked. The New Testament is plain: the adopted children of a forgiving God will obviously show their Father's great characteristic of forgiveness.

As I admitted at the start of this chapter, this is not an easy

topic. Actually, I suspect that Jesus knew this was the most difficult part of his model prayer. My reason for saying this is
because at the end of it (Matthew 6:14–15) Jesus repeats the
point with emphasis: 'If you forgive those who sin against you,
your heavenly Father will forgive you. But if you refuse to
forgive others, your Father will not forgive your sins.' Elsewhere
Jesus frequently talks in the strongest language about the need
for forgiveness. In Matthew 18:21–22 we read how Peter came
to Jesus and asked him, 'Lord, how often should I forgive
someone who sins against me? Seven times?' He probably
thought he was being generous with the seven times. If so, Jesus'
answer must have shocked him. ' "No!" Jesus replied, "seventy
times seven!" ' The number Jesus gives here would have been
symbolic. Rather than imply that Peter could cease forgiving on
the 491st offence, Jesus was suggesting that forgiveness must be
extended on an indefinite basis. Did he ever say anything harder?

---

**If we refuse to forgive ... we are sawing off the
branch we are sitting on.**

---

We need to remind ourselves of the way Jesus links God's
forgiveness and our forgiveness in the Lord's Prayer. It is worth
noting that modern versions of this part of the Lord's Prayer
are significantly stronger than the traditional version's 'forgive
us . . . as we forgive'. They put the action of forgiveness in the
past tense, as in the New Living Translation's 'forgive us our
sins, just as we have forgiven those who have sinned against us'.
The link Jesus makes is so strong that it seems to imply that if
we do not forgive we will not be forgiven. That's something
that should not be ignored. As I said earlier, what he means

here is not that God forgives us because we forgive others. What he does say is that if we are not able to forgive, then it seems that we know so little about forgiveness that there must be a question as to whether we have indeed come into a right relationship with God. If we are unforgiving, is it perhaps because we have not really trusted the forgiveness of God? To be so wonderfully and generously forgiven by God is something that must overflow into our own lives. If we refuse to forgive, we are denying the principle of forgiveness; we are sawing off the branch we are sitting on.

Before we go any further we need to think about what forgiveness means.

## What does it mean to forgive others?

The goal of forgiveness is to try to handle a hurt or an injury that someone has inflicted on us so that our relationship with them can be restored. But what does it mean to forgive? 'Forgive and forget' says the proverb, though interestingly such advice does not come from the Bible. Indeed, if forgiving means forgetting, how could any parent forgive a drunk driver who had killed their child? They certainly couldn't forget it.

Let me try to make some helpful suggestions here. You would be best advised not to consider them as final and definite answers to what can be an extraordinarily difficult problem but as principles that may help you work through issues in your life.

### Forgiveness is a decision, not an emotion

One of the problems we face in the area of forgiveness is that we confuse what is a decision of our minds with what is a feeling of our hearts. There is a danger that we think forgiveness is all about us having good emotions about someone who has done something dreadful to us. Unsurprisingly, if we think of forgiveness like that, we are in danger of dismissing it as being totally impractical and probably impossible.

The idea that we can be confused between an emotion and a decision is something that is better known in the area of love. Our culture today thinks that love is something you feel; it is a warm, gushing and wonderful emotion. The Bible's view of love, however, is different: it is first and foremost a decision to seek the very best for the other person whatever it may cost. To show Christian love to a vomit-stained drug addict is not primarily to feel your heart beating with a glowing affection towards them; it is a hard-headed determination to help them and do everything you can for their well-being. I think that the situation with forgiveness is very similar. Initially, at least, it is an act of the will. It is a decision we take. We *personally* no longer wish to hate or punish the person who has hurt us; we *personally* choose to end the matter and take no further action or retribution over a grievance. I have put 'personally' in italics because, as we shall see, there may be cases where we want the legal processes of punishment or compensation to continue.

Although forgiveness is initially a decision, it does not stay at that. Once the decision is made, then I believe we are able, with God's help, to ensure that our emotions of anger, hatred and bitterness fall in line with our decision. Forgiveness of the will should eventually become forgiveness of the heart. Of course in some cases the healing of the hurtful emotions may take years. I suspect that the first step on that road is always the same: we choose to forgive.

Finally here, let me point out that forgiveness can be seen as the negative aspect of love. Forgiveness is the decision not to wish to return harm to someone; love is the decision to wish the best for someone and to help them achieve it. Certainly unless we forgive we cannot begin to love in the Bible's sense of the word.

### Forgiveness is a work for which we need God's help

Every act of forgiveness – from making the decision to carrying out the action – needs God's help. Even to decide to forgive may require a work of God's Spirit softening our hearts and strengthening our determination. A major part of the act of forgiving for Christians is to take the matter to God for his healing touch. This is especially so where we have suffered some real and deep hurt. There we may need a powerful working of God's Spirit in our lives to achieve any sort of forgiveness. Let me suggest that you go openly and honestly to God with your hurts and anger, and ask him to give you the strength to forgive. You may find that to bury every trace of the anger and bitterness completely may require you to take the matter to God on more than one occasion. The prayerful support of others throughout the process may be of enormous help.

### Forgiveness is a process rather than the work of a moment

Every so often we read of people who have managed to forgive dreadful acts against them or their family in a way that we cannot imagine possible. Sometimes, however, we find this sort of extraordinary forgiveness more daunting than encouraging. We need to realise that where the injury is major, any sort of deep and complete forgiveness may take years.

The initial stage of forgiveness is to make the decision to forgive. There, to use an image, you take all the hurt and bitterness you feel, kill it and, as if it were a corpse, bury it. You have declared the grievance now dead and buried, and it is out of the way. Now you can deal with the person who hurt you without the corpse of your injury getting in between you. You are not forgetting that the hurt occurred (you know where you buried it and you may even have laid a mental tombstone over it), but it takes no further part in proceedings. Of course, the problem here is that there is always the danger that the hurt will be dug up. It may need either determination on your part or the power of the Holy Spirit (or probably both) for you not to exhume the remains.

The final stage of full forgiveness is reached when there has been forgiveness of the emotions as well. Although sadness may remain, any bitterness is now gone. Now there is no longer any possibility of digging up what you buried. Grass has grown over the grave where you placed the hurt, and you have forgotten where you put the spade. You still remember what happened, but it's in the past. To reach this final stage where the hurt is fully resolved and full forgiveness has taken place can take many years, especially where there has been a deep injury. Sadly, for some people it may never happen and it is all too easy to take bitterness and anger to the grave. Instead, we should take it to Jesus.

### Forgiveness is a lot easier with repentance

When a relationship has been broken, forgiveness is the act of healing. We can think of it as if the hurt or injury were some deep gap that has appeared between two towns, severing communications. To forgive is to make a bridge across that chasm and to restore the links. If the person who has injured you has repented, and he or she has genuinely said that they are sorry, then it is as if they were building the bridge from their side as well. The task of restoring the relationship is a lot easier. A bridge can be built from one side alone, but it is a lot easier if both sides work at building it.

Where someone who has hurt you refuses to repent or, even worse, brings the matter up again or repeats the offence, then reaching the stage of full and final forgiveness may be very hard indeed.

### Forgiveness does not mean ignoring justice

To forgive a wrong is not the same as condoning that wrong. Take, for example, theft. If someone has stolen from me and I forgive them, I am not saying that what they did is right. I am simply forgiving their wrong actions against me personally. It is helpful to remember that what Jesus is talking about here is personal forgiveness. He is hardly recommending that society abolish its legal system by bringing in total forgiveness! In fact later in Matthew (18:15–18) Jesus lays down rules for church discipline. I see no discrepancy, in theory, in a Christian forgiving a mugger but then testifying against them in court; or a Christian forgiving the driver who injured them, while at the same time seeking from them fair compensation for injuries.

### Forgiveness does not always mean forgetting everything

The heart of forgiveness is the burying of the bitterness and anger over what you have suffered. You are trying to put the hurt behind you. Nevertheless, to forget *everything* may be naïvety rather than holiness. For instance, as the owner of a shop, you might personally forgive an employee who has stolen from you. However, there would be no contradiction in you simultaneously removing that person from a position where such an abuse could occur again. You want reconciliation and restoration of the relationship, but you must also show wisdom. In some cases you may have to say, 'I forgive you, I really truly do desire the best for you and I bear you no ill will or malice, but I do not trust you.'

## Have we forgiven?

Finally, in the light of these points, let me raise a serious question: Have we truly forgiven those who have hurt us? It is all too easy to say of someone who has injured us, 'Oh yes, of course I forgive them,' but still harbour deep in our hearts some secret ill will.

In fact the best indicator of whether we have truly forgiven someone is how we feel about them now. Listen to the following phrases. Can you hear yourself saying anything like them?

'I suppose I do hold it against her really. I feel she still owes me an apology. Justice was not done.'

'Oh I don't wish him dead. But reading his obituary would give me pleasure.'

'That accident served him right. After what he did to me, he had it coming to him.'

'I've still got a score to settle with him.'

'I tell you what, after what she said to me I'm never going out of my way to help *her*.'

If we can hear ourselves saying any of these things or something similar about a particular person, then what we have called forgiveness may not be forgiveness at all. It may simply be the pretence of forgiveness. We may need to go back to the beginning and make that decision to forgive again. We should also seek God's strength to help us keep to it.

The test of forgiveness is being able to genuinely wish whoever it was that injured us well and want only the best for them. If we were to hear that they had won some prize or honour, become happily married, had wonderful children or had anything good like that happen to them, we would rejoice with them. If we can truly say that, then forgiveness has taken place. Equally, if we hear that they have suffered some misfortune or illness and can grieve for them without the slightest thought of 'serves them right!', then forgiveness has taken place.

I know that these are hard tests but we need to apply them, and where we fail we need to repent and to seek God's forgiveness and the power of the Holy Spirit to completely forgive. Realising God's forgiveness ourselves should give us more motivation to forgive others.

## WHY WE SHOULD FORGIVE OTHERS

Forgiveness is a tough option. It is simple enough to say wisely about some dispute, 'Oh, if only they'd forgive each other,' but to those involved in it, forgiving may be the very hardest of things to do. We must be very careful not to be glib about forgiveness. If we ever make it sound effortless we are in danger of inflicting more hurt on those who are already hurting.

Owing to the fact that forgiveness is so tough, we need to look at all the arguments that there are for it.

## Why forgiveness matters

Before we come to specifically Christian aspects of forgiveness, let me talk about forgiveness generally. Outside Christian circles, forgiveness is not a widely used concept today. In fact if you ever see a newspaper headline such as ' "I forgive attacker" says victim', most likely you will find that the person who is doing the forgiving is a Christian. The loss of forgiveness as a virtue in our culture probably explains why there is so much anger and hate around. We may prize tolerance and acceptance, but forgiveness is far less popular. Forgiveness is, however, infinitely more important.

The fact that forgiveness is scarce today is unfortunate because failing to forgive carries with it a high cost. For instance, without forgiveness any wrongs that are committed go on to produce further wrongs. We tend to think of hurts or injustices as being like stones dropped into a pond; sooner or later the ripples die away and all is forgotten. But human nature is not like that. One wrong committed against someone almost certainly generates another and often stronger wrong in retaliation. This in turn provokes another even stronger response and so on. Soon an uncontrolled chain reaction has started as grudges are repaid by angry words, and angry words by angry actions. Without forgiveness things soon spiral out of control. You have only to look at any one of the world's trouble spots such as Northern Ireland or the Middle East to see examples of this.

People often say that time is a great healer, yet without forgiveness there is little that even time can do. Most of us know communities where there are people who refuse to speak to each other and have not done so for years. When you enquire about the reason for the squabble you sometimes find out that the problem goes back to some hasty words uttered a whole generation before. In fact, sometimes the feud continues even

---

**No one can bear hatred or bitterness for more than a short time without being scarred by it.**

---

though no one can now remember what started it in the first place. And we all know about nations where simmering hatreds go back centuries. Anger and bitterness produce a fire that can consume anything and will burn on and on; only forgiveness can quench such flames.

If we fail to forgive, the results of our lack of forgiveness may not just be among other people. No one can bear hatred or bitterness for more than a short time without being scarred by it. Anger borne against others inevitably spills over into the bearer's life. When we fail to forgive some wrong done to us it is almost as though we hammer an anchor into the ground at that point in our lives. As a result, the world moves on but we stay fixed, locked to the past. Sometimes you meet people whose lives have been twisted by some event where, long ago, they were badly wronged. Yet by holding on to that grievance, by gnawing on it, their suffering has just grown over the years. Far from reducing the hurt, time has magnified it.

There are lots of good common-sense reasons for forgiveness. For Christians, there are many more still.

## Why Christians in particular must forgive

The Bible does not put forgiveness on the Advanced Syllabus of Applied Christianity, with a little warning that it is only to be attempted by experienced Christians. It is for all of Jesus' followers, all of the time. Let me try and briefly list the reasons why, as Christians, we should forgive.

### We are commanded to forgive

Quite simply we are under orders by Jesus to forgive and to show love even to those who hate and despise us. In fact, Jesus' insistence on forgiveness is almost alarming. We are commanded to forgive our enemies (Matthew 5:43–44; Luke 6:27–36).

### We are to imitate Jesus Christ

As those who have been called into God's family we are to imitate our Lord Jesus Christ. His whole life illustrated forgiveness, most of all the manner of his death. On the cross he said, 'Father, forgive these people, because they don't know what they are doing' (Luke 23:34). The gift of the Holy Spirit helps us grow into the likeness of Christ and part of his role is to enable us to forgive.

### We have been forgiven ourselves for much worse

We need to remember that we ourselves are sinners who have been forgiven in a most extraordinary and costly way by God. As we have seen, Jesus spoke very strongly about any of his followers who failed to forgive. His most dramatic expression of this was in a powerful parable that he told just after Peter had asked him how many times he was to forgive someone:

'For this reason, the Kingdom of Heaven can be compared to a king who decided to bring his accounts up to date with servants who had borrowed money from him. In the process, one of his debtors was brought in who owed him millions of pounds. He couldn't pay, so the king ordered that he, his wife, his children, and everything he had be sold to pay the debt. But the man fell down before the king and begged him, "Oh, sir, be patient with me, and I will pay it all." Then the king was filled with pity for him, and he released him and forgave his debt.

'But when the man left the king, he went to a fellow servant who owed him a few thousand pounds. He grabbed him by the throat and demanded instant payment. His fellow servant fell down before him and begged for a little more time. "Be patient and I will pay it," he pleaded. But his creditor wouldn't wait. He had the man arrested and jailed until the debt could be paid in full.

'When some of the other servants saw this, they were very upset. They went to the king and told him what had happened. Then the king called in the man he had forgiven and said, "You evil servant! I forgave you that tremendous debt because you pleaded with me. Shouldn't you have mercy on your fellow servant, just as I had mercy on you?" Then the angry king sent the man to prison until he had paid every penny.

'That's what my heavenly Father will do to you if you refuse to forgive your brothers and sisters in your heart.' (Matthew 18:23–35)

Paul sums up this principle in Colossians 3:13: 'You must make allowance for each other's faults and forgive the person who offends you. Remember, the Lord forgave you, so you must forgive others.'

Can we who have been forgiven by Christ's death not show mercy to others?

*A failure to forgive reflects negatively on our own forgiveness*

I touched on this earlier but it bears repeating. God's forgiveness and our forgiveness of others are linked strongly in the Lord's Prayer and elsewhere in the New Testament. If God has forgiven us, then that rich forgiveness should overflow into our dealings with other people. If we do not forgive, we are denying the very principle of forgiveness that has given us peace with God.

*There are spiritual consequences if we fail to forgive*

If we fail to forgive, there are inevitable spiritual repercussions. A failure to forgive must hinder our fellowship with God. If we nurse bitterness in our heart, it is difficult for us to have a right relationship with God.

A failure to forgive also results in the door being opened for evil. In Ephesians 4:25–27 Paul says, 'So put away all falsehood and "tell your neighbour the truth" because we belong to each other. And "don't sin by letting anger gain control over you." Don't let the sun go down while you are still angry, for anger gives a mighty foothold to the Devil.' Paul implies that a lack of forgiveness can allow the devil to enter our lives. A similar thought lies behind Paul's comment in 2 Corinthians 2:10–11: 'When you forgive this man, I forgive him, too. And when I forgive him (for whatever is to be forgiven), I do so with Christ's authority for your benefit, so that Satan will not outsmart us. For we are very familiar with his evil schemes.' It is almost as though when we are angry the devil comes alongside us and says, 'If you let me, I'll help you get even.'

*We should remember that God is just and that in the end justice will be done*

For the Christian the challenge of forgiving someone is enormously helped by the fact that we believe God is Judge of us all. The idea that we can leave justice in the hands of someone who knows all the facts and can judge with perfect fairness is very liberating. Mind you, even here we probably ought to be careful. It is good for us to remember that in the case of the crucifixion, the greatest injustice in history, Jesus Christ asked his Father to forgive his executioners (Luke 23:34).

*We should remember that God is sovereign and can use even bad things for our good*

Part of our anger over many injustices can be because we feel robbed. That robbery may be of something like money, promotion or property, or it may be of something less visible like honour or happiness. Yet the Bible teaches that God is sovereign over events and he can use even evil incidents for the long-term good of his children. In the Old Testament Joseph saw God's hand in all the trials he underwent. In Genesis 50:20 he says to his brothers, 'As far as I am concerned, God turned into good what you meant for evil.' In the New Testament Paul says in Romans 8:28, 'And we know that God causes everything to work together for the good of those who love God and are called according to his purpose for them.' This adds a new perspective to suffering and injustice. God can compensate us, even in this life, for loss. Such a belief is, of course, a long way from the trite and often insulting 'everything will work out for the best' that you sometimes hear. What we can say as we struggle to forgive some hurt is that our loving heavenly Father has allowed this event and he can use it to make us more like Christ. Whatever we may think about the origin of suffering in the universe, the practical point is that God is capable of turning around even bad things inflicted on us to our good and his glory.

*We should remember that a failure to forgive will do us no good*

Revenge is a great temptation but offers little long-term satisfaction. To refuse to forgive is to allow an emotional cancer to grow in our life. Forgiveness may be painful and revenge may be sweet, but forgiveness will do us lasting good, while revenge will do us only lasting harm.

## PRACTICAL IMPLICATIONS

### Think about how you pray

Let me suggest some principles that may help us when we come to pray about forgiveness.

#### Be honest with God

It is easy to be deceived in the area of forgiveness. For instance, we may admit that we are sinners before God (isn't everybody?), but we can sometimes be wary about *specifically* confessing where and how we have sinned. So every time we pray this prayer, when we come to this point 'and forgive us our sins, just as we have forgiven those who have sinned against us' we need to pause for a moment to ask God to show us precisely where we have failed him so that we can deal with it. Equally, when we think about other people we need to ask who we *spe-*

*cifically* need to forgive. If we are honest and open, God will, through his Holy Spirit, put his finger on specific incidents or occasions we need to bring to him. The danger with being dishonest with God is not that we fool him (how could we?) but rather that our prayers cease to be real; they just become empty words.

As with so many things there are two opposing dangers here. One is to fail to believe in the reality of sin so that you come to God with a careless attitude, under the impression that what you have done wrong is not really all that serious. Trivialising sin, and all that God has done for us in Christ, is a recipe for disaster. The other and opposite danger is to fail to believe in the reality of forgiveness. Here you become obsessed by your failings and, as a result, fall into a guilt-haunted, joyless Christianity. The Bible teaches that there is both a terrible reality to sin and a glorious reality to forgiveness. That is one reason, among many, why reading the Bible is so important: it helps us strike the right balance. If we read it, we will see that while Christians are sinners they are also God's loved and forgiven children.

## Keep short accounts with God

Don't let things fester. As we have seen, the Lord's Prayer is very much a day-by-day prayer and it makes sense to evaluate our need to be forgiven and to forgive on a daily basis. We should regularly bring before God those things we've done wrong during the past day and ask his forgiveness for them. At the same time we should also bring before him those whom we need to forgive and ask that, through the Holy Spirit, he gives us the strength to freely and fully forgive them.

## *Treat repentance seriously*

'Repent' and 'repentance' are words we use often, but we frequently drain them of their meaning. We can easily think of repentance as being a decision or an emotion that takes place in our heads, having nothing to do with our actions. The fact is, repentance is more than saying sorry and promising not to do it again. Repentance should involve us asking God to show us if there is anything we can do to make up for what we have done wrong. In case you hadn't realised it, it's not much good saying sorry to God for a life of robbery if you intend to keep hold of the proceeds. Repentance isn't just words; it also involves actions. When we come to God asking for forgiveness, we need to be ready to do what he says. The story of Zacchaeus in the Bible (Luke 19:1–10) illustrates what the effects of repentance should be: an urgent desire to make recompense and restitution.

## *Believe in forgiveness*

Christianity treats forgiveness as a certainty rather than a vague hope. Yet it is a certainty that many Christians seem to have forgotten. They may believe that in principle Christianity is about forgiveness; they just find it very hard to feel that it is true for them.

This is one reason why it's important that we talk to God about specific issues rather than just use generalised 'Lord, I'm a sinner' prayers. Guilt feelings can come from the devil as well as being prompted by the Holy Spirit. In fact I suspect the evil one rather enjoys the spectacle of miserable Christians doubting whether God has actually forgiven them. So how can we tell the difference? Is it the devil making us feel guilty, or is it the Holy Spirit convicting us? One helpful rule centres on this area of specifics. The devil delights in general guilt and in making Christians feel all-over worthless, generally rubbish and complete failures. His only concern is for us to be miserable, despairing and ineffectual. In contrast, the Holy Spirit is concerned with conviction – giving us the knowledge that, in a specific area or over some specific issue, we have fallen short of God's standard. The purpose of conviction is always that we will repent and seek forgiveness.

When you come to God for forgiveness, ask him to deal with specific issues. Some people find that writing these items down is very helpful. One advantage of dealing in specifics is that when, as is all too likely, some matter in your past surfaces and you feel accused over it, you can remind yourself that in this specific case you have been forgiven by God and that is the end of the matter. The wonderful thing about God's forgiveness to us through Jesus Christ is that it allows us to say that our past is forgiven, however dark it may be. Remember that if God has said we are forgiven, it would be wrong to deny it.

Finally, as you think about how wonderful it is to be forgiven, remember that God wants the forgiveness he has shown you to spill over into your relationship with others. As you have been forgiven, so forgive others. Forgiveness is something that ought to be splendidly contagious. Remember that troubling parable of the unforgiving debtor? Wouldn't it be great to rewrite the ending?

But when the man left the king, he went joyfully to a fellow servant who owed him a few thousand pounds. He put his arm around him, hugged him and said, 'Remember the few thousand you owe me?'

His fellow servant went pale and gulped. 'Er well . . .'

But the man who had been forgiven by the king said, 'Relax, my friend! I have just been forgiven millions. So I have torn up your bill. I'm forgetting all about it.'

'You're forgetting my bill?' gasped his fellow servant, his eyes nearly popping out of his head.

'What bill?' said the man who had been forgiven by the king, and together they walked away as friends.

Know that you are generously forgiven. As a result, generously forgive.

## Think about how you live

In this area of forgiveness Christians can make an enormous impact on society. As I mentioned earlier, anger, rage and bitterness are all too common. Without forgiveness there are simply no mechanisms for people to deal with hurts. Christians can stand out as different by the way they deal with injustices.

That is why a failure to forgive in the church is so catastrophic. The apostle Paul, for example, used very strong language to the Corinthians when they failed to forgive each other and went to law instead (1 Corinthians 6:1–8). We are supposed to set an example.

Before I briefly sketch out some principles on forgiveness, let me say that I am here outlining general rules that I believe apply to the majority of cases. However, I am well aware that special situations exist, especially where the hurts run deep, for example where we have been the victim of some kind of abuse. Here, as in many other areas, it may be a good idea to seek advice from a mature Christian or church leader you can trust.

## Pardon promptly

It is best to seek and give forgiveness as soon as possible. Remember the passage from Ephesians 4:26–27: 'And "don't sin by letting anger gain control over you." Don't let the sun go down while you are still angry, for anger gives a mighty foothold to the Devil.' Paul was concerned that forgiveness should be given before nightfall; in other words, he wanted it fast. There is sound sense in this. If you delay forgiveness, any hurt or offence will multiply in your mind. As you sit there and think about the grievance, you will find yourself saying something like, 'This is really the last straw!' Very soon you can get yourself into the state of mind in which forgiveness is almost impossible.

## Pardon privately

Another good rule is to try to minimise the number of people involved and, if you can, sort it out between just the two of you. In Matthew 18:15 Jesus says, 'If another believer sins against you, go privately and point out the fault. If the other person listens and confesses it, you have won that person back.' Again, this makes sound sense. Once a dispute goes public, it becomes very complicated. Other people decide to weigh in and score points, honour and pride become important and it becomes harder for either side to back down.

## Pardon profusely

It is tempting to offer forgiveness with strings attached: 'I will forgive you, if you do this or that.' You cannot make demands with forgiveness. If you include demands then you are not for-giving, you are negotiating a settlement. That may be better than fighting, but it's not forgiveness. Forgive freely and generously.

### Pardon permanently

You cannot give forgiveness and then take it away later. A con-ditional forgiveness is not really forgiveness. As we have seen, one of the blessings of forgiveness is that it enables you to put the past behind and move on. Provisional forgiveness keeps you rooted to the past.

### Pardon prudently

The aim of forgiveness should not be just to end some dispute; it should be to do good to the one you're trying to be recon-ciled to. This means that forgiveness must be intelligent. For instance, suppose you catch some local alcoholic breaking into your house. You could of course just let them go and tell them they are forgiven. However, you might very well decide that it is in their best long-term interest for the police to be called. These are hard cases but that's the point. You need to think about how you forgive in order to apply forgiveness in the wisest way.

### Pardon practically

We also need to work out how we can apply forgiveness prac-tically. Forgiveness should not simply be an attitude of the heart; it should also be an attitude expressed in our lives. The best sign that we have actually forgiven someone is that we decide to do good to them. Remember, Matthew used the word 'debts' here and this really meant 'sins', but it could easily also be real debts. Indeed, if there was someone who owed you a thousand pounds but couldn't pay, I am not sure how you could forgive them without waiving their debt. Forgiveness ought to extend as far as our bank accounts.

It is an interesting fact that there is an entire book in the New Testament whose theme is forgiveness. This is the book of Philemon and it is a short personal letter by Paul to a slave owner, asking that his runaway slave now be forgiven and accepted back. In many ways it is the most unusual book in the New Testament – a purely personal letter on what is really a rather private matter. However, it is almost as if the Holy Spirit, in inspiring the writing of the New Testament, felt that forgiveness was such an important matter that it was important to include a practical example. Forgiveness must be practical.

## Pardon persistently

What if your attempt to try and forgive is rejected? What if insult is added to the original injury? What if the person who hurt you says, 'You may forgive me but I will never forgive you'? To use the bridge image again, what if there is no attempt to rebuild the bridge from the other side?

Well, I think we ought to do all we can and then probably a bit more. Jesus himself gives an attention-grabbing illustration in Matthew 5:23–24: 'So if you are standing before the altar in the Temple, offering a sacrifice to God, and you suddenly remember that someone has something against you, leave your sacrifice there beside the altar. Go and be reconciled to that person. Then come and offer your sacrifice to God.' Notice that the problem is not that *we* have something against someone else but that *they* hold a grievance against us.

Nevertheless, Jesus says we are to leave the 'Temple' and go to them (which presumably then could have been a day's journey or more) and be reconciled to them. Jesus seems to be saying that we build the bridge over to them, even if they do not want it. If they demolish it, we try and build it again and again. These are, I know, hard words, but it seems to me Jesus taught that we are to extend the hand of forgiveness as long as we can.

Here, as with other problems regarding forgiveness, it may be worth seeking advice if your efforts at reconciliation reach a dead end.

### Pardon prayerfully

I have made the point that prayer without action is pointless. The alternative is also true. For forgiveness to occur it is best surrounded by prayer. Forgiveness is not a natural possession of any of us. Many people today think that if they forgive they will be seen as weak and having been forced to give in. For repentance and forgiveness to take place we need God to soften the hearts of all involved, including our own.

### Practise pardoning

Finally, forgiveness is something we have to learn. The best way of learning is to practise forgiveness in small areas. Next time someone cuts in on you when you're driving, or borrows your coffee mug in the office without your permission, then forgive them. If you practise in the little areas then when the big crises come upon you, you are far more likely to be able to respond in a forgiving manner.

## QUESTIONS

- Why does revenge seem so much more attractive than forgiveness?
- Do you see forgiveness as an act or an emotion?
- Which do you find the hardest to forgive – an insult to yourself or an insult to someone you care for?
- If you were to picture what God does with your sins, would you think it was like (a) tearing up a bill or (b) storing the record away out of sight (but not beyond recall) in a filing cabinet? Which is closest to the biblical image?
- Does forgiveness overflow out of your life or does God have to squeeze it out? How do we learn to live lives where forgiveness comes more easily?

# 7

# Protection

*And lead us not into temptation; but deliver us from evil.*
(Traditional)

*And don't let us yield to temptation,*
*but deliver us from the evil one.*
(New Living Translation)

This petition in the Lord's Prayer talks about the battle against evil. In the first part of the petition we ask that we might win our spiritual battles; in the second we ask that we may be protected from the devil, our spiritual enemy.

This petition covers an area of life that few people today, other than Christians, take seriously. In fact, if you were to try and find the meaning of the word 'temptation' from the media you would probably conclude that it was merely having the desire to eat chocolate when you were slimming or wanting to buy things when you didn't have enough money. As for trying to find the meaning of the word 'devil', I suspect you would be totally confused. You would probably get the image of some sort of cartoon figure – a man dressed in red with horns, a pitchfork and a pointed tail, who was a sort of negative version of Santa Claus. This ignorance of the non-Christian world has spilled over into the lives of some Christians, where the idea that we are engaged in battle against hostile spiritual powers seems to be largely ignored.

In a situation as confused as this, it is especially important that we look carefully at the Bible and check out what God has said.

Let me deal with the two big issues in this petition, temptation and the evil one, in turn.

## TEMPTATION AND TESTING

Some Christians not only have problems with defeating temptation, they also have problems in understanding the concept of temptation. If you have often prayed the traditional version of the Lord's Prayer where you ask not to be led into temptation, then I can understand your confusion. After all, you could easily believe from this that it is God who is doing the tempting and that we are asking him to spare us from it.

In fact there are two issues here: what 'temptation' means and what exactly it is that we are praying about. In fact the word translated as 'temptation' could also mean 'testing'. And, on the surface at least, the two words seem to represent totally different things. 'Temptation' is a negative word, indicating a destructive desire by the tempter to encourage us to sin, to break God's laws and to turn away from our relationship with him. So does God tempt us? James 1:13–14 answers this question: 'And remember, no one who wants to do wrong should ever say, "God is tempting me." God is never tempted to do wrong, and he never tempts anyone else either. Temptation comes from the lure of our own evil desires.' So then God does not tempt.

In contrast to 'temptation', the word 'test' is much more positive. To test is to find out the state of an object or to prove something. The goal of testing is good; for example, think of someone who has passed their driving test or whose antique has been certified, after testing, as highly valuable. Testing in some shape or form is a common part of life: factories have quality control assessments; accounts have auditors; schools have inspectors. In every case the test is to determine whether there has been progress or whether something is of a genuine or high quality. We can apply this idea of testing very widely so that, for example, you could easily hear someone talk about the first test of their relationship, or how the course was a real test.

The Bible is plain that God tests his children (Genesis 22:1; Deuteronomy 8:2, 16). This testing is not to help God decide how we are doing (he already knows that); it is for our benefit and the benefit of those around us. In this context, you could say that God is enlarging our faith by stretching it. His intention is that our relationship with him can grow and mature. In fact it is quite common to hear those who have been Christians for a long period of time say how they grew in their faith through some particular test or trial, whether it was illness, bereavement, unemployment or something else.

So what is the relationship between temptation and testing? I think they are basically two ways of describing the same thing, but from different perspectives. Let's take a hypothetical case. Ruth's ageing and argumentative mother comes to stay with her for two weeks. Ruth needs to talk some things through with her mum, but faces the challenge of staying calm and not having a blazing row with her. From God's point of view these two weeks are a test for Ruth so that through it her faith will be strengthened and matured. You could easily envisage that if all goes well she may be able to say, 'I really learned a lot about being patient when Mum came to stay. It was only the power, presence and peace of the Holy Spirit that enabled me to get through.' From the devil's point of view, however, these two weeks offer the opportunity not of testing, but of tempting. If he can get Ruth to snap at her mother and have an almighty row, then he has won a victory. What Ruth faces therefore is both a test and a temptation. If she manages to love her mother through this difficult fortnight, then Ruth will look back on this as a test that she successfully passed and one in which her faith grew. If, on the other hand, she gives in to anger and bitterness, she will look back on this as a temptation that she gave in to.

I have to confess here that there are a number of areas that I want to pass over. Does God use the temptation of the devil for his testing? Certainly that seems to be the issue in Job (1:6–12). Or is it that God's testing process is hijacked by the devil? Couldn't God have made a form of testing where we couldn't fail? These are fascinating theological and philosophical questions that lead us eventually to why God allowed evil into his universe in the first place, but as fascinating as they are, I'm not sure they are actually very useful. For one thing they may be questions to which only God knows the answers. More importantly, the problem we face with evil and temptation is not the academic one of how it originated, but the very real and practical one of how to defeat it.

So what exactly are we praying about with respect to temptation or testing? The New Living Translation captures it well: 'And don't let us yield to temptation'. We cannot avoid challenging times, but we should pray that when they come upon us, we pass the test rather than fall for the temptation.

THE TEMPTER

## The devil, evil and the supernatural

The older versions of the Lord's Prayer talk about us being delivered 'from evil'. It is now, I think, generally recognised that what Jesus is referring to here is not some abstract principle or force of evil, but rather to a specific being or person whom he calls 'the evil one' and whom the Bible elsewhere calls the devil or Satan.

The first thing to say here is that we must not ignore this statement. There are widespread, diluted interpretations of the Bible that view evil as merely some sort of failure to meet the standards set by society, and 'the devil' as no more than a quaint figure of speech. However, if we take the Lord's Prayer seriously we have to disagree with such views because we ask in it to be delivered from the evil one. Here as elsewhere, Bible-based, authentic Christianity is supernatural Christianity. It believes in a real and supernatural God and also in a no less real and supernatural devil who opposes God and his works.

I am aware that there are some people who find the idea of a supernatural evil hard to swallow. I would want to respond with four points.

1. To state that you believe in the biblical view of evil and the devil is *not* to say that you automatically believe in every supernatural belief going around, from lucky charms to

out-of-body experiences. Most Christians are very sceptical about many of the wild, bizarre and wacky ideas that can be found under the headings of the occult or the paranormal. This has always been the case. A fascinating but often overlooked fact of history is that it was the revival of a Bible-based Christianity in the fifteenth and sixteenth centuries in Western Europe that saw the end of magic and superstition and allowed the rise of science. Now to say this is not to say that everything in the occult is harmless superstition; some beliefs and practices are very harmful and it is undoubtedly best to steer clear of the whole thing. Believing in Jesus and being open to any and every sort of superstitious belief are two very different things.

2. When you examine the state of the world, the idea that there are malevolent and evil spiritual forces nudging events and people seems hard to dismiss. In fact as we look back on the twentieth century, with its wars, genocides and ethnic cleansings, its unparalleled destruction of the environment and its persistent abuse of technology, it would be irrational to confidently dismiss the concept of a supernatural evil. As a cynic remarked, 'It's not believing in an evil devil I find a problem; it's believing in a good God.'

3. It is important to remember that outside a relatively small number of people, most of whom have lived in Western Europe and North America from 1900 onwards, the vast majority of human beings who have ever existed have believed in the existence of a spiritual world with both good and evil forces. The fact remains that in global and historical terms, scepticism about the supernatural is very much a minority belief.

4. One objection to a belief in the devil or a supernatural evil
   influence made by some people is that it offers human
   beings a moral excuse. What they are worried about is the
   sort of thing we have all seen reported under such newspaper headlines as '"Devil made me do it" says axe murderer'. Actually this sort of 'blame-the-devil' excuse is never
   seen in the Bible. Even if the devil has a role in either insti-
   gating or encouraging evil, the responsibility always lies
   with individual human beings. Incidentally, if the papers
   reported things fairly, the alternative headline '"God
   stopped me from doing it" says potential murderer' would
   be much more frequent!

Arising from the last point is something very important and
all Christians, especially new ones, need reminding of it. Not
everything that is evil or strange is a direct manifestation of the
devil. For instance, take a Christian who suddenly starts to
suffer moods of despair and depression. Some people might
immediately consider that this was caused by demonic attack.
While this might be a possibility, the wisest approach would
first be to assume that it was an ordinary physical illness, probably brought about by an imbalance in the brain's delicate
chemistry. That is not to say that we shouldn't pray for them.
Of course we should pray, asking for the Holy Spirit to fill them
and give them peace. However, the advice of skilled doctors or
counsellors may be more appropriate than an exorcism!
Deciding in this and many other cases whether you are dealing
with a supernatural attack by the devil or 'just' a psychological
or physical phenomenon is actually very hard. That is why wise
Christian leadership is essential when dealing with possible

supernatural manifestations of evil. Some over-zealous and irresponsible claims of demonic activity have only served to help the devil, by making Christians seem foolish.

No, although the idea of a devil and the demonic might be unpalatable to some people and may at times have been abused, it cannot be removed from the pages of the Bible. Jesus was under no doubt that a devil and a supernatural evil existed and I see no option but for those who follow Jesus to believe the same.

## The nature of the devil

I want to try and summarise what the Bible says about the devil, but before I do that I ought to outline something of what the Bible teaches about the supernatural. Although it never describes the supernatural world in any detailed or methodical way, the outline seems fairly plain. From various passages it seems clear that in addition to humanity, God also created angels – intelligent beings who are not physical creatures in the sense we are. These spiritual beings, some of them very powerful, are now divided into those who are aligned with God and those who, having rebelled, are in opposition to him. Those angels opposed to God are termed 'demons' and the chief demon is the devil or Satan. Incidentally, most of the popular imagery about demons, angels and the devil comes from sources other than the Bible. Efforts of painters such as Michelangelo and poets such as Milton to portray Satan and demons may have given rise to great works of art, but they cannot be relied on as accurate sources of information.

The Bible (our only reliable source here) does not say a great deal about Satan. This is probably because as a rebellious angel the devil is a being infinitely inferior to God. This is worth remembering.

I want to sketch out some of the characteristics of the devil, first looking at those aspects of his nature that should make us wary of him, and second balancing that by looking at those aspects that should encourage us. It is vital that we avoid the extreme errors of either fear or over-confidence.

## The devil is a powerful enemy

In addition to retaining his powers as an angel, he holds considerable influence over this world. Three times Jesus called the devil the 'prince of this world' (John 12:31; 14:30; 16:11). Indeed, Satan felt able to offer the world to Jesus if he would worship him (Luke 4:5–7). Paul terms him 'the god of this evil world' (2 Corinthians 4:4) and in Ephesians refers to the devil and his demonic servants in these terms: 'For we are not fighting against people made of flesh and blood, but against the evil rulers and authorities of the unseen world, against those mighty powers of darkness who rule this world, and against wicked spirits in the heavenly realms' (Ephesians 6:12).

## The devil is a malicious enemy

Satan is a hate-filled being who loathes what is good and longs for the destruction of God's people and God's kingdom (see, for example, Matthew 13:24–30; 36–43). Jesus says of the devil that he was 'a murderer from the beginning' (John 8:44). There are no deals or treaties that can be negotiated with him. Think of all the evil characters you have seen in movies, remove any trace of any virtues such as wit, humour or nobility, put them together and you have a faint picture of the character of the devil.

### *The devil is a* ruthless *enemy*

There is a relentless and merciless fury about his work. He is untiring in his schemes and although he may pause in his attacks, his hatred never ceases. Once he has found a weakness you may be sure he will pursue it. One thing is clear: there is nowhere this side of heaven where you can be safe from temptation; for example, you can be tempted in church and you can be tempted while reading your Bible. In 1 Peter 5:8 we read, 'Be careful! Watch out for attacks from the Devil, your great enemy. He prowls around like a roaring lion, looking for some victim to devour.' The testimony of Christians in the 2,000 years since Peter wrote this is that the devil's hatred and appetite have never decreased.

### *The devil is an* intelligent *enemy*

There are many sorts of temptation, and the devil, knowing our weaknesses, is capable of using the most appropriate one to exploit them. He is equally adept at trying to turn almost any situation to his benefit. For example, in prosperity he will tempt us to rely on ourselves and to forget God; in poverty he will tempt us to despair and to deny our faith. In Genesis 3 we see how, as the serpent in the Garden of Eden, the first assault of the devil on the human race was marked by great cunning and skill. With a series of lies and half-truths, he sowed seeds of doubt and wrong desire in Eve's mind. He has repeated this pattern endlessly ever since. He can quote the Bible if it suits him.

## *The devil is a* deceitful *enemy*

Jesus said of him that he 'has always hated the truth', that he is 'a liar' and that he is 'the father of lies' (John 8:44). Nothing has changed. His tactics today often involve deception. So, for example, many temptations are presented as acts of little consequence that we can always choose to walk away from later. In reality, many of them are one-way doors through which no return is possible. Equally, the devil often makes us think that if we only give in to this or that temptation then lasting happiness will be ours; in reality we find that the happiness is fleeting.

## *The devil is a* crafty *enemy*

Paul says, 'Even Satan can disguise himself as an angel of light' (2 Corinthians 11:14) and his temptations are far more subtle than we imagine. His temptations are rarely direct attacks but are far more frequently indirect, secret or underhand assaults that arouse no suspicions until the moment it is too late. For example, someone may find themselves involved in a large-scale deliberate fraud and, looking back, see how by imperceptible steps they were led from half-truths through lies to full-blown deception.

## *The devil is an enemy* with allies

The Bible is plain that sin has negatively affected both the world we live in and our own minds, hearts and bodies. The result is that our own inclination is to find evil attractive rather than repulsive. Adultery becomes a 'bit of an adventure' rather than the sordid betrayal of a faithful partner; workplace theft becomes 'helping myself' rather than robbery of a trusting employer. In other words, when the devil tempts us our minds aid him.

In short the devil is a formidable enemy – influential, hateful, crafty and often disguised. Yet against all these facts must be placed other teachings of the Bible that give a much-needed balance to our picture.

### *The devil has only limited power*

The devil's power has limits. For one thing he is an angel and not God. For another, the Bible is plain that whatever power the devil has, it can only be used with God's permission. The clearest example of this in the Bible seems to be in the first two chapters of the Old Testament book of Job, where God gives Satan strictly limited powers to test a godly man, Job, by suffering. Frankly here we touch on matters such as freewill and why God allows evil that are not easy for us to understand. Practically, the main point is that God remains in charge. God has set out limits to what the devil can do to us. Ultimately, our lives are in God's hands.

### *The devil is a defeated enemy*

From the Bible we learn that Jesus has won the decisive victory over the devil through his death on the cross (see, for example, John 12:31; Colossians 2:15). Although the devil remains a formidable enemy with considerable power, he has been defeated.

### *The devil is a doomed enemy*

At the Second Coming, when Christ returns in glory, the devil and all his forces will be judged and destroyed by God

(2 Thessalonians 2:8; Revelation 20:10). The devil's time is limited and his ultimate destiny sealed.

### God has given his people power to defeat the devil

God provides a way of escape when the devil tempts: 'And God is faithful. He will keep the temptation from becoming so strong that you can't stand up against it. When you are tempted, he will show you a way out so that you will not give in to it' (1 Corinthians 10:13). If resisted, the devil will flee (James 4:7). Above all, because believers have the Holy Spirit in them, they are more powerful than the evil one: 'But you belong to God, my dear children. You have already won your fight with these false prophets, because the Spirit who lives in you is greater than the spirit who lives in the world' (1 John 4:4). On this subject, Romans 16:20 makes a great promise: 'The God of peace will soon crush Satan under your feet.'

### God has ordered us to battle against the devil's forces

In the light of what we have learned about the devil's power, it might be tempting to think that the Christian's best strategy is to keep a low profile and stay out of high-risk situations. This is not the advice of the New Testament and it certainly was not the strategy of the leaders of the early church. Amid the warnings about the devil, there are also encouragements to take the offensive against him and his works. For instance, in 2 Corinthians 10:3–5 we read the following:

> We are human, but we don't wage war with human plans and methods. We use God's mighty weapons, not mere worldly weapons, to knock down the Devil's strongholds. With these

weapons we break down every proud argument that keeps people from knowing God. With these weapons we conquer their rebellious ideas, and we teach them to obey Christ.

Paul is telling the Corinthians to preach the good news aggressively, to take the church forward and to rescue people from the devil's clutches. Of course, it was this attitude that allowed the explosive growth of Christianity after the resurrection. Jesus had told his followers to take the light of the gospel into the darkest parts of the world and his followers were simply obeying orders. I am cautious about making this point in case I encourage the reckless. The balance of the New Testament, though, must be proclaimed; yes we face an enemy, but our task is not to leave him alone but, under God's guidance and with God's power, to take from the devil and his forces what he has claimed for himself and give it to Christ. We don't engage him directly by name, or in prayer; we advance against him by proclaiming the good news of Jesus and standing for the truth.

With these things in mind, let me now turn to talk about the battle we fight; in particular to the enemy's strategy and the ways in which we should counter it.

## THE BATTLE

### The devil's strategy

Jesus' temptations give us an insight into the devil's strategy. Luke 3 tells the story. Notice how Jesus is led by the Holy Spirit to the place where he is tempted. He is the only one this happens to. For the rest of us, God leads us away from temptation.

Notice about the temptations that the devil begins tempting with questions: 'If you are the Son of God . . .' As in Eden the devil begs questions of doubt over God's good word. Jesus has just heard God's voice publicly declare him to be the Son, and now, immediately after, the devil brings a question to Jesus' mind over whether he is or not. The devil will question God's truth over us, particularly about our identity. The devil knows that if he can get us to doubt our identity he has got to the most treasured thing we have and are.

All the temptations seem to be trying to knock Jesus from going the way of the cross: to do miracles, to make life easier for himself, turning stones to bread, to achieve the position of lordship by missing out the cross and simply bowing down, and by getting huge numbers of followers by performing amazing public stunts. Jesus rejects all these. Interestingly, apart from the obvious one about bowing down in front of the devil, they are things that aren't wrong in and of themselves. Jesus will perform miracles making food and drink for people. What is wrong is that in this case they divert him from the path of the cross. The line behind seems to be 'If you are the Son of God you shouldn't have to go through agony and pain – you should have it easy'. If the devil tempted Jesus in this way, it is likely he will use the same tactics on us. He will beg questions about whether we truly are God's children and he will tempt us to take routes other than the cross.

In 2 Corinthians 2:9–11 Paul describes how discipline in the Corinthian church is to be administered in order that '. . . Satan will not outsmart us. For we are very familiar with his evil schemes.' He was making the point that it is sensible to be aware of the devil's strategy and his methods. It is impossible to outline all the tricks the devil employs; nevertheless, there are some general methods he uses repeatedly and it would be foolish not to mention these.

The overall aim of the devil is plain. He maliciously wants to undo all that Christ has done. Where Christ has given freedom, the devil wants to bring slavery; where Christ has brought joy, he wants to bring despair, and where Christ has brought peace, he wants to bring hatred. With respect to individual Christians, he wants either to destroy us or to so weaken us that we are no longer effective servants of Christ and his kingdom. His aim for the church is the same: to destroy it or to totally neutralise its power.

There are many weapons the devil can use against Christians, but before I talk about them I want to point out that much of his work is not a direct attack against us, but towards the under-mining of our defences. Christians who have a close, regular and living relationship with God present the greatest obstacle to the devil because they are heavily protected. The powerful presence of the Holy Spirit, a close fellowship with Jesus Christ; regular habits of reading the Bible, prayer and worship, all make his attacks more difficult. As a result, a priority of the devil is the weakening of those defences.

## How the devil undermines our defences

Let me outline some of the means the devil uses to weaken us.

## The devil encourages complacency

If we can be made to think that we are secure and above temp-tation, then it is easy for us to relax, drop our defences, untie our anchor and drift from God. Ironically, it is often at times when our lives are peaceful and untroubled by want or illness that we let our guard slip. Comfortable times are often the most dangerous. We need to remember that, in this life, Christians are never off duty.

Equally, the devil is happy for people to profess Christianity as long as they do not allow it to change their behaviour. This complacency can affect churches too. The way most churches today lack any real enthusiasm to reach out to those around them with the good news of Jesus Christ is a tragic example of this sort of collective complacency.

## The devil encourages isolation

Another tactic the devil uses to undermine the resistance of Christians is to encourage them to become isolated. Christians are more protected when they are in a close and caring fellowship and are praying for one another. In conflict, Roman soldiers often used large oblong shields that could overlap with those of the men beside them. The result was what they called 'the tortoise', an almost impenetrable armour wall against which attack was very difficult. Christians praying for one another provide a similar overlapping protec-tion. I have no doubt that it is at least partly for this reason that the devil loves to encourage difficulties within churches, so that people leave and decide to go it alone. As we have seen elsewhere in the Lord's Prayer, the best model for the

Christian life is to be part of a church fellowship and in the context of spiritual warfare this makes very good sense. Many churches also encourage the development of additional small-scale fellowship units, often as Bible study or home groups. These smaller groups of anything between three and a dozen people can provide the sort of close, personal and confidential support that Sunday church services cannot give. Obviously some Christians become isolated through no fault of their own, perhaps as a result of a posting in work or being housebound. In this case it is good to try and find things that will act as some sort of compensation. These include helpful Christian books or tapes. Be warned: isolation is dangerous and if at all possible it is best avoided.

### The devil encourages distractions

At the time of the D-Day landings in 1944, the Allies put a great deal of effort into persuading Hitler's forces that the invasion would be in a different place to the planned Normandy sites. The reason, of course, was so that the defensive forces would be moved away from where the landing would be. The devil has used a similar strategy for years. He seems to delight in having Christians focus on one issue as being 'the battleground for me' or where 'we as a church

---

**In your efforts to guard the front door, make sure you haven't left the back door wide open.**

---

must stand firm' and then launching an attack in quite another area. For instance, what you believe and what you do as a Christian are both vitally important. There have fre-

quently been individuals (and churches) who have so emphasised the importance of correct beliefs that they have been left
wide open in the area of correct practices. And vice versa.
Remember, even if there are specific struggles that God has
called you to devote your efforts to, be wary of allowing weaknesses to develop elsewhere, as these can be exploited. In your
efforts to guard the front door, make sure you haven't left the
back door wide open.

## The weapons the devil uses

The devil aims to do with us what he did with Adam and Eve
at the start of human history: to make us doubt and disobey
God, so that we will rebel against him. Here I want to highlight two of the most important weapons he uses.

### 1. The devil will deny truth

The devil is a deceitful enemy and will always attack truth,
either by telling outright lies or by twisting the facts. Let me
give two areas where his deception is major.

*First, the devil will deny the truth of what sin is.* He may, for
instance, encourage us to create a mental league table of sins
with at least three different categories: 'serious sins', 'not so
serious sins' and 'things that we feel bad about but which are
not really sins at all'. Unless we are ruthlessly honest, what will
be included in 'serious sins' will be violence, adultery and theft
– probably things that we ourselves are not prone to. Our own
sins are much more likely to be put in the 'not really sin' category. By managing to avoid 'serious sins', we may fool ourselves that we are doing all right, or even that we are not
actually sinful. Yet if we allow the Bible to be the standard of

what is sin and what is not sin, then things start to look different. For one thing, as Jesus pointed out in the Sermon on the Mount, thoughts can be just as sinful as actions. Indeed, as he spelled out in Matthew 5, anger is mental violence, lust is mental adultery and greed is mental theft. For another thing, some things we do not tend to think of as serious sins, or even as sins at all, are condemned in the Bible. For example, in Colossians 3:5–9 Paul lists the following as sins: sexual sin, impurity, lust, shameful desires, greed (which he equates with idolatry), anger, rage, malicious behaviour, slander, dirty language and lying. This broad range of sins, some of which we might consider minor, should be a warning to us.

*Second, the devil will deny the truth of who God is.* He delights in twisting our thinking about God and how we relate to him. In Genesis 3 we read how he did this at the dawn of human history, persuading Eve that God was not the generous and loving figure he had claimed to be. You see, if the devil can make us think that our relationship with God is some sort of heavy burden, then he has won a major victory. After all, if we think that God is a cruel and unfair master, then we may feel that rebellion against him is justified and even an act of liberation. In the same area the devil delights in sowing seeds of doubt so that we start asking ourselves questions such as 'Does God really love me?' and 'Can I be assured that I am forgiven?' There are all sorts of distortions he can introduce. For instance, he may try to make us believe that the normal Christian life is one long tale of triumph, ecstatic joy and spectacular achievement. If our lives are anything else (which will almost certainly be the case), he suggests this shows how we are 'Grade B' Christians. He may even darkly hint that we are possibly not even Christians at all.

## 2. The devil discourages

Perhaps one of the devil's most powerful weapons is discouragement. He takes pleasure in making us think that the Christian life is impossible. He will draw attention to our failures and suggest that we have failed so badly that God cannot possibly use us. The same tactic works at a church level, where he may be responsible for suggesting that some mission venture is impossible or that a perfectly valid church project is totally unrealistic. I believe the devil is especially anxious to discourage people from trying to rob him of what he has acquired, through their efforts to tell other people about Jesus, to bring the liberating good news of Christ into the world and to spread the kingdom. I think one of the commonest phrases the devil slips into Christians' minds and words today is simply: 'Why bother?' Apathy is a close cousin of discouragement. Remember that sin consists not just of doing things that are wrong, but of failing to do things that are right.

One common area of discouragement lies with temptation itself. Here the devil's strategy is to suggest that because you are being tempted you are a failure. A moment's thought will suggest that this is nonsense; after all, Jesus was tempted! In 1 Corinthians 10:13 Paul warns that temptation is common to us all. Actually, if you are never tempted, you might want to wonder why! In warfare the only soldiers who are not attacked are those who have either surrendered or are already dead. While giving in to temptation is sin, temptation itself is not. We are not tempted because we are evil; we are tempted because we are human.

The ultimate form of discouragement is despair. Here the

Christian reaches a point of such darkness and gloom that they feel a total failure and conclude that the only reasonable thing to do is to give up. This is, of course, admitting defeat and handing the devil victory.

## Our defence

The following few points may be helpful in this area of spiritual warfare.

### Avoid temptation

If you believe in the serious nature of spiritual warfare you should realise that temptation is not something you play with. However attractive and harmless it may appear, we need to remember that it is utterly poisonous and deadly. It is worth remembering that far better people than you or I have wrecked their faith by playing with temptation, only to suddenly find that they were in far too deep to get out.

I recommend that you take care over your thought life. The prevailing view in our society today is that thoughts do not matter. After all, who sees them or is hurt by them? We are told that if we want to let our mind dwell upon hatred or adultery, that's fine. It's our business. The Bible's advice, however, is very different; not only is the imagining of evil wrong but it is sowing seeds that may well grow into words or actions that will be bitterly regretted. Paul wrote this to Christians in Rome: 'Let the Lord Jesus Christ take control of you, and don't think of ways to indulge your evil desires' (Romans 13:14). Deal ruthlessly with your thought life.

Even if you face something that is only a potential temptation, give it as wide a margin as you can. Equally, as soon as you are aware that you are faced with a temptation, turn your back on it quickly. 'I'll deal with it in a moment,' has been too many people's last words before committing some dreadful sin. To pray against temptation and yet to rush into situations where temptations may occur is to thrust your fingers into the fire and then pray they will not be burned. Be accountable. However embarrassing it might be, tell someone about what you are struggling with.

## *Prepare for temptation*

Avoid temptation, but remember that even if you do not seek temptation, it will find you. Temptation is inevitable for anyone who is serious about following Jesus. Therefore, be prepared! I quoted earlier Peter's warning in 1 Peter 5:8 about the devil being 'a roaring lion, looking for some victim to devour'. The attacks will come, often when you least expect them and often from a surprising angle.

The first step to prepare ourselves for fighting temptation is to make sure we are walking in God's ways and that we are filled with God's Spirit. It is ridiculous to live a careless and sloppy Christian life and then suddenly expect to triumph over temptation. As in human warfare, training and discipline count. We need to make sure that our Christian lives are in the best possible shape.

How do we live Christian lives that provide the greatest resistance to the devil? To answer that properly would require a longer book. What I can say is that there are two aspects to living an effective Christian life.

The first aspect is that we are to examine our lives and get rid of anything that might hinder us spiritually. The Bible, particularly the letters of the New Testament, are full of commands to put away sin, to get rid of evil desires and to reject all that is evil. Just to give one example, Paul addressing the Ephesian church says,

> But that isn't what you were taught when you learned about Christ. Since you have heard all about him and have learned the truth that is in Jesus, throw off your old evil nature and your former way of life, which is rotten through and through, full of lust and deception. Instead, there must be a spiritual renewal of your thoughts and attitudes. (Ephesians 4:20–23)

We need to evaluate our lives. Is there anything in them that belongs to our old life from before we were converted? Have we desires, habits or even possessions that we would be far better off without? Let's get rid of them.

The second aspect is that we are to work hard at allowing God to renew and reshape our lives. It is not enough to get rid of things that are wrong; that just leaves a vacuum. As Paul implied at the end of the passage from Ephesians quoted above, we must also have a spiritual renewal of our thoughts and attitudes. The New Testament is full of similar instructions for us to renew our lives, to live according to the Spirit and to imitate Christ. It is a challenging exercise to get a copy of the New Testament and underline or highlight all the positive commands on how we are to live as followers of Jesus. It is even more challenging to try and live them out.

I also need to say that as part of our preparation to fight temptation, we need to consider our individual Christian lives in the context of our fellowship with other believers. As we have been reminded elsewhere in the Lord's Prayer, we are not just individuals; it is vital to have a supportive fellowship. Both your church and your home group, if you have one, can play a part here. In addition to these, many people also have a friend with whom they can develop a close spiritual relationship and with whom they can pray and share problems in confidence. The sort of person you need for this is a Christian you respect – someone you can be accountable to, whom you can call on at any time and who will not abuse their position with you. Of course, even if we do have such multiple levels of fellowship supporting us then that is no excuse for complacency. Even the strongest locks are no use if you leave the key in the door!

To restate what ought to be obvious: pray. Ask God that when temptation comes you will not yield but will resist, and that when the evil one attacks, you will be delivered from him.

*Know your weaknesses*

Linked with being prepared for temptation is the necessity of knowing our own weaknesses. The devil is not foolish enough to attack where we are strongest; instead he unerringly seeks out and attacks those places where we are susceptible. It is therefore as well that we find them before he does. Of course, our weaknesses vary and what one Christian may be able to resist may be harmful to another. The wise Christian will know what they can, and cannot, do safely. Where they realise they have a weakness, they will steer clear of any situation where that vulnerability might become a liability.

The biggest weakness of all is to believe that you have no weaknesses. Pride or over-confidence can be disastrous. Paul warns about this in his first letter to the Corinthians: 'If you think you are standing strong, be careful, for you, too, may fall into the same sin' (1 Corinthians 10:12).

Remember that against such a powerful spiritual enemy we have no defences on our own. However, Jesus Christ has already defeated the devil and at his word the evil one must flee. When the devil personally attacks us, the wisest strategy is to refer him to our Master and Lord, Jesus Christ. The one who has died to save us from the devil's power will also come to our aid.

### Hold firm to the truth

Deception is one of the devil's chief weapons, and as a result it is vital that we hold firm to the truth. Once we lose sight of what the truth is, we are in very serious trouble indeed. The mind is the control centre of our lives, and if the devil is allowed free range within it, then disaster is inevitable. If on the other hand we can focus our mind on God's will by reading the Bible and praying, then we will be better able to resist the attacks of the evil one. Further sound advice from Paul is found in Romans 12:2, where he says, 'Don't copy the behaviour and customs of this world, but let God transform you into a new person by changing the way you think.'

The importance of having minds that are centred on God's truth is emphasised by a striking illustration given by Paul in his letter to the Ephesians. There he gives a command to the church to be 'strong with the Lord's mighty power' and to 'put on all of God's armour so that you will be able to stand firm against all strategies and tricks of the Devil' (Ephesians 6:10–11). Paul then goes on to describe all the elements of the armour of God, such as the breastplate of God's righteousness, the shoes of peace, the shield of faith, the helmet of salvation and the sword of the Spirit. A key element though is the 'belt of truth', a reference to the wide leather belt that held the rest of the soldier's armour together and which protected the lower part of the body. Without this belt, the rest of the armour would be useless and the soldier would have been vulnerable. In the same way truth is vital; without it our defences will fall apart. Truth lets us see the real issues and allows us to expose all the lies that the devil uses to try to entice us into sin. Holding to the truth is a key part of fighting against the evil one.

### Fight temptation

In one of his plays, the flamboyant and tragic nineteenth-century writer Oscar Wilde had one of his characters say, 'I can resist anything except temptation.' Many people adopt the same principle. At the first sign of temptation they raise their hands and surrender. The advice of the Bible is exactly the opposite; it is to resist. Paul's command to the Ephesians was 'to stand firm'. In the same passage he goes on to say, 'Use every piece of God's armour to resist the enemy in the time of evil, so that after the battle you will still be standing firm. Stand your ground, putting on the sturdy belt of truth and the body armour of God's righteousness' (Ephesians 6:13–14). Paul here makes it plain that we are not to flee but rather to stand our ground. The apostle James echoes this advice: 'So humble yourselves before God. Resist the Devil, and he will flee from you' (James 4:7–8). In other words, we are to put up a fight.

In fact, unless we are prepared to fight temptation, the idea that we have any ethical standards or morality is a total sham. We may say wise and good things about what is right and wrong but those words are going to be very empty if we deny them by our actions. Without resistance to evil, any morality we have is simply wishful thinking. The first hint of pressure – and it will not be long coming – will cause us to cave in.

As the following story illustrates, once we give in to one temptation, we will give in to others. A student once asked his university lecturer if he would raise his marks 10 per cent for twenty thousand pounds. The lecturer hesitated, thought about what he could do with all that money and agreed. The student then said, 'And would you give me the 10 per cent raise for fifty pounds?'

'What sort of person do you think I am?' snapped back the lecturer angrily.

'Oh,' came the answer, 'you've already told me what sort of person you are. Now I'm just negotiating the price.'

### Depend on God's resources

But how do we resist?

From the start it is very important to remember that we cannot defeat Satan in our own strength. To attempt to defy the devil in our own wisdom and power is an act of extraordinary foolishness. In fact the very point of this part of the Lord's Prayer is that we are asking for God's strength and power from a position of weakness. We are dependent on God to give food and to grant forgiveness; we are equally dependent on him to aid us in spiritual battles. Only by confessing our own weakness and by seeking Christ's help can we overcome the evil one.

Let me suggest three important things to remember.

1. *Christ has already defeated Satan.* Through Christ's death on the cross, the devil has already been defeated. Proof of this victory was given by Jesus' resurrection. Paul says of Jesus' victory, 'In this way, God disarmed the evil rulers and authorities. He shamed them publicly by his victory over them on the cross of Christ' (Colossians 2:15). One day, as the book of Revelation graphically portrays, Jesus will complete that defeat by utterly destroying the devil. In the meantime, although still capable of causing immense damage, the devil's power is limited. As Christians are linked to Christ through his Spirit, we also share in Christ's victory.

2. *Christ sympathises with those who are tempted.* We ought to be encouraged by the fact that Jesus knows what we face. He himself underwent the severest temptation, notably in the wilderness (Matthew 4:1–11; Mark 1:12–13; Luke 4:1–13) and also in the Garden of Gethsemane (Matthew 26:36–46; Mark 14:32–41; Luke 22:39–46). So when we are tempted, we know that Christ can understand what we are going through. We can never say to Jesus, 'You don't know what it's like.' The letter to the Hebrews expresses this truth: 'Since he [Jesus] himself has gone through suffering and temptation, he is able to help us when we are being tempted' (Hebrews 2:18; see also Hebrews 4:15).

3. *Christ strengthens those who are tempted.* Christ's support for his people is more than just sympathy; it is also strength. In heaven he prays for us (Hebrews 7:25) and through his Spirit in us we are given strength to stand firm against temptation. In 2 Thessalonians 3:3 Paul expresses the following confident hope: 'But the Lord is faithful; he will make you strong and guard you from the evil one.' There

are also promises that when temptation comes, God will provide us an escape route: 'And God is faithful. He will keep the temptation from becoming so strong that you can't stand up against it. When you are tempted, he will show you a way out so that you will not give in to it' (1 Corinthians 10:13).

## Two final encouragements

Let me conclude by saying two more things about temptation that I hope will be encouragements.

First, remember that the battle will not go on for ever. Sometimes it may seem impossible to continue a struggle against temptation; you cannot see how you can go on a minute longer. There are two things to bear in mind here. One is to fight the battle moment by moment and step by step. The battle you face *now* is all-important; tomorrow's battles can be fought tomorrow. The other is to remember that sooner or later all our battles against temptation will be ended. It is a bit like being a player in a football match; by the closing minutes of the second half you are desperately tired but you keep going. You hang on, sustained by the knowledge that at any second the referee's final whistle will blow. For all Christians the truth is that one day, either by our earthly lives coming to an end or by Christ's coming again, our struggles with sin and temptation will be over. And then we will be face to face with Christ and eternally safe from temptation and Satan.

Second, let me remind you that as Christians we serve a forgiving God and, as we saw earlier in the Lord's Prayer, we believe in forgiveness. If you have fallen in your struggle against temptation, then turn to God in repentance and faith and ask him to forgive you and to give you the power to overcome the sin you are grappling with. You may have lost a battle; you have not yet lost the war. What you must avoid at all costs is the despair that says, 'I have failed utterly and all I can do is give up.' As always, the Bible is very helpful here with its honest portrayal of people like David, Elijah and Peter who all, in one way or another, failed God and yet he was able to use them again. (You can read about them in 2 Samuel 11–12, 1 Kings 18–19 and John 18, 21.) Of course this is no excuse to give in to sin. But if you have failed in temptation and have repented of your failure, receive God's forgiveness and allow him to comfort you.

## PRACTICAL IMPLICATIONS

### Think about how you pray

I have already mentioned the importance of prayer in the previous pages, but I want to remind you of the importance of prayer in spiritual warfare. Prayer is one of the greatest of spiritual weapons. Through it we access for ourselves and for others God's mighty power both to defend us from attack and to enable us to overcome the works and influence of the devil. Let me list some things to consider.

- When you pray, remind yourself that in this life you live not in friendly or even neutral territory. You are in a hostile world. You need to pray accordingly. Pray for strength and protection around you, pray persistently and do not slacken.

Pray for wisdom and discernment in avoiding places and situations where you may be exposed to temptation.

- When you pray, ask God to give you wisdom and insight to understand the strategy and tricks of the devil. Pray that you will be clear-minded and not distracted.

- When you pray, ask that God would show you your weaknesses and reveal to you how you can deal with them so that your defences will be built up.

- When you pray, ask God to give you strength through his Spirit so that not only can you resist the temptations of the devil, but you can wrestle successfully with his forces to bring glory to Christ.

- When you pray, ask that others might also be given what you have prayed for yourself. Remember that your prayers may make a difference between them stumbling into shame or sorrow, or triumphing gloriously. Become intercessors on behalf of your brothers and sisters in Christ. Remember, the emphasis in the Lord's Prayer is plural. It is meant to be a prayer that Christians pray together as a community of believers.

- When you pray, pray for people around you, for your workplace, your home, your town or country. Then pray about the world and especially those places where it seems the devil is having a major influence.

- Finally, when you pray, pray in faith that God will answer. Of course, in your expectancy allow God the freedom to answer your prayer his way. Remember that God's answer may not come at the time you expected or in the manner you assumed it would.

## Think about how you live

Again, much of what I have already written in this chapter is about how we live. To truly realise that we are all part of a continuous invisible spiritual conflict fought for the highest stakes should revolutionise how we live. In becoming a Christian you are no longer a neutral party – you have signed up with God's forces. Paul's words to Timothy have relevance to all Christians: 'And as Christ's soldier, do not let yourself become tied up in the affairs of this life, for then you cannot satisfy the one who has enlisted you in his army' (2 Timothy 2:4).

Believe in the existence of the devil, but don't see him everywhere; be aware of him, but don't fear him. When you feel attacked by him, don't try to deal with him directly. Simply refer him to your elder brother, Jesus.

As we pray, so we are to live. In all you do, be careful to avoid evil or anything that might lead to evil. Be careful not just about actions and words, but also thoughts. Be alert for dangerous situations and where at all possible avoid them.

Remember that you do not live in this hostile world alone. You are part of the body of Christ. Your brothers and sisters in Jesus are also struggling with temptation. Do what you can to help them; your prayers may give them the protection they need. Equally, do not be a means of temptation to them. For instance, you may not have a problem with drinking alcohol, going to certain types of movie or balancing ambition and a Christian commitment. Younger Christians might; don't trip them up by your example. As the apostle Paul once said, 'But you must be careful with this freedom of yours. Do not cause a brother or sister with a weaker conscience to stumble' (1 Corinthians 8:9).

Finally, remember that prayer and action go together. After all, your practical deeds may be the answer to someone else's prayer for protection against temptation. It is frankly hypocritical to pray, for example, that God will help someone overcome their problem with loneliness and not visit them or invite them round for a meal. Equally, to pray for someone's stress levels without thinking whether you can help them, makes a mockery of prayer. As elsewhere, we need to make sure that we have not created a gap between the spiritual and the physical through which we can fall.

## QUESTIONS

- When you think of temptation, what are the first things that come to mind? Are these most prominent temptations the most dangerous ones?
- On what fronts do you feel the devil is attacking you? What can you do about that?
- If you had a friend who was not a follower of Jesus and who was fascinated by the occult, what would you say to him or her? Would they be easier to talk to than someone who believes that there is no supernatural at all?
- Which is more dangerous: to be frivolous about the devil or to be fearful? How do we strike a balance?

# 8
# Perspective

*For thine is the kingdom, the power and the glory, for ever and ever. Amen.*
(Traditional)

*For yours is the Kingdom and the power and the glory for ever. Amen.*
(New Living Translation footnote)

This final phrase of the Lord's Prayer does not appear in the earliest manuscripts of the New Testament and, as a result, most modern translations place it as a footnote. Nevertheless, I think that we should consider it as part of our model for praying for four reasons.

1. It appears to be a very early addition to the Lord's Prayer; it was almost certainly used by the church within a hundred years of Jesus giving the prayer to the disciples.
2. Jewish prayers of Jesus' time generally ended with some sort of blessing to God, so it is perfectly probable that Jesus expected his followers to conclude the prayer with words similar to these.
3. I also think it extremely unlikely that they would have

ended the prayer on the rather downbeat note of 'protect us from the evil one'. Here, as elsewhere, the devil doesn't have the last word!

4. This ending takes us back from spiritual warfare to praise. It is a model of the exultant, jubilant and hopeful note upon which all our prayers ought to end.

By praying this ending, or something modelled on it, we enclose our own concerns within a framework of praise to God. I covered praising God in Chapter 3 and will not repeat what I said there. Here I want to point out how vital it is for us to leave our prayers on a note of praise like this. Only this sort of confident expectant praise will put our concerns and our lives into the right perspective.

Let's look in turn at 'the kingdom', 'the power' and 'the glory' and then, last of all, think about that significant little word 'Amen'.

## THE KINGDOM: THE PRIORITY OF OUR LIVES

God's kingdom is *for ever*! That is an awesome thought. Everything else – all worldly powers, business empires and political regimes – will pass away, but the kingdom of God will go on for ever.

We need to remind ourselves of this again and again as we conclude our prayers. We live in a world of unprecedented choice. We have almost limitless opportunities around us: supermarkets stocked with thousands of brands, a hundred television channels, a thousand things to read, a whole world to take our holidays in. Endless products and services compete for our money, and a never-ending number of activities struggle for our limited time. We all have to make priorities all the time. But how do we set them?

There are two extreme ways of setting priorities. One is to actually set no overall priority at all. This way you simply drift, allowing yourself to be tugged this way and that by advertising or the pressures of society. You respond to the loudest 'Buy This!' advertisement by purchasing; to the smartest 'Support This!' campaign by voting; to the most seductive 'Watch This!' trailer by switching on. There are always new sets of pressures. After a thousand such pulls and pushes you are simply left exhausted. The other extreme is to set your own overall priority and, with total determination, pursue it relentlessly to the exclusion of everything else. Whether it is your work or wealth, everything else takes second place or is trampled underfoot. Nothing else matters.

For Christians, the kingdom is to be our main priority. As we think about how we live, how we spend our money and our time, what we must always remind ourselves of is the kingdom. God has placed us here on this earth and allocated us all the time we have to serve him and work for the extension of his rule and authority. We may be successful in life, perhaps reaching the top of our profession, winning an Olympic gold medal, producing some great work of art. These things are worthwhile, but the really pressing question we must all ask ourselves is: What are we doing for the kingdom of God?

This is not to say that we should have such a narrow view of the kingdom of God that we think only full-time Christian workers can serve it fully. By bringing God's standards to bear wherever he has called us – at home, in the office or in the classroom – we are serving the kingdom of God. Making the kingdom our priority means being open to God as the King of our lives to allow him to use us wherever he puts us.

Hanging over all our decisions in this life, whether we work in a classroom, café or church, should be this one priority: the extension of the kingdom of God. This may sound noble and self-sacrificing, but actually it is the other way around. After all, if the kingdom of God is going to last for ever, isn't it worth investing in?

## THE POWER: THE STRENGTH OF OUR LIVES

The reference to power here is a reminder that God's strength is eternal. It is also a vital reminder at the end of our prayers that everything we do is in God's strength.

Negatively, this should remind us that we can never turn round to God and say, 'Lord, look at what I have done for you!' We can never boast that we have put God in our debt. All we have ever done and all we will ever do for the kingdom is because of God's strength working in us.

Positively, this is a tremendous encouragement to us as we face the challenge of living out our prayers in our lives. God's awesome strength, that unbelievably vast energy that keeps the universe going, is the power that is available for us. In Ephesians 3:20 Paul writes, 'Now glory be to God! By his mighty power at work within us, he is able to accomplish infinitely more than we would ever dare to ask or hope.'

God's Spirit is the gift God gives to all Christians and it is only through that almighty Spirit that we can hope to live out the sort of life that brings honour to God. Here, and nowhere else, is the power to praise God and to work for the kingdom, to forgive and to overcome sin and the devil.

## THE GLORY: THE PURPOSE OF OUR LIVES

The reference to glory reminds us of the ultimate purpose of what we are and what we do. God – Father, Son and Spirit – is to be glorified in our thoughts, words and actions. It is God who is to be praised – not us. In a culture where seeking our own glory is a normal priority, this is a desperately needed perspective. God alone must be glorified. If what we do results in us being forgotten and God's kingdom and the name of Jesus being praised, then that is sufficient. Contrary to what everyone else says, we do not have to make a name for ourselves. God expects us only to lift up the name of Jesus!

'For yours is the Kingdom and the power and the glory' puts our lives – past, present and future – into true perspective. In the light of the eternal kingdom of the all-powerful and eternal God, all our hopes and fears, ambitions and cares seem small and temporary matters.

I'll come back to this at the end of this chapter, but first let's look at the very final word of the prayer, 'Amen'.

## AMEN

'Amen' is a curious little word. A Hebrew word that was brought into the Greek of the New Testament, it basically means 'be true'. It was a word that Jews used to confirm or agree with something, whether it was a prayer, a blessing or even a curse. In modern English speech, it means 'so be it', 'let it be so' or even 'let what we have said be binding on us'. By using the word 'Amen' at the end of a prayer, a Jew of Jesus' day would have been making that prayer their own.

Let me give you two illustrations of what 'Amen' means.

1. 'Amen' is like the signature at the end of a contract. Until a contract is signed it is merely words and has no value. It is only binding when a signature is put at the end. By signing our name we are saying, 'I personally approve of what has just been written. I agree with it and I allow myself to be bound by its terms.' So when we say 'Amen' we are adding our verbal signature to what we have just prayed.
2. 'Amen' is like raising your hand to vote for a motion. Imagine you are in some tense meeting of a small committee and a proposal is set out. Finally it comes to those crucial words, 'All those in favour?' By raising your hand you are saying, 'I vote for this – I am committed to it.'

So saying 'Amen' at the end of a prayer is a decisive act of commitment to or agreement with what has been prayed. It is not to be done lightly.

We need also to remember that the word 'Amen' has very practical implications attached to it. By signing a contract with your signature, you are committing yourself to a course of action. You are bound by it. You cannot subsequently back out and say, 'Oh, that isn't what I meant!'

There is, however, another aspect to 'Amen'. If 'Amen' is an expression of our commitment or agreement to God's purposes, there is also in it a longing that God's purposes will be worked out. By saying 'Amen' we are asking God to bring what we have prayed to fulfilment. We are saying to God, 'Let your name be honoured!' or 'Let your kingdom come!' or 'Let your will be done!'

At the end of the book of Revelation, in the very last verse of the Bible, the apostle John catches this note perfectly: 'He who is the faithful witness to all these things says, "Yes, I am coming soon!" Amen! Come, Lord Jesus!' When we say 'Amen' to the Lord's Prayer what we are praying is similar: 'Lord, fulfil your promises. Make them come true. Bring in your eternal kingdom, power and glory! And soon.'

Next time you say a prayer, the Lord's Prayer or any other prayer, don't just say 'Amen'. Pause and ask yourself some questions: Am I really serious about what I have said? Am I prepared to commit myself to what I have prayed? Am I prepared to live in a way that is consistent with my prayer? Am I prepared for God to answer my prayers? If you are, and only if you are, then go ahead and say 'Amen'.

## THE FUTURE: GOD'S KINGDOM, GOD'S POWER, GOD'S GLORY

What we have thought about in this last chapter are very important matters; about God being the priority, the strength and the purpose of our lives. However, I believe that they are only part of what this closing sentence is about. Read it again and, if you can, read it aloud: 'For yours is the Kingdom and the power and the glory for ever. Amen.'

In praying these words we are speaking not just to our minds, but to our hearts as well. In looking at the Lord's Prayer we have inevitably concentrated on the words of our prayers.

Yet prayer, and especially praising prayer, is more than words and it can reach deeper than logic or reason. This phrase is one that strikes to the very depths of what we are. Of course, every word of it is true, yet it is more than that; it touches the heart and the spirit. 'For yours is the Kingdom and the power and the glory for ever' is a statement that should, when we pray it, make our spirits rise and our pulse quicken. This is a phrase that we want to be sung by the best music group or choir and orchestra imaginable, at a volume to rattle the church roof and windows. In praying these words we are making a glorious and wonderful statement of praise about God. *Yours,* we say, is the kingdom, the power and the glory. *Yours* is all the majesty and authority, *yours* is all the power and energy, and *yours* is all the magnificence and splendour. God, we cry, it all belongs to you. By saying these words we are humbly and joyfully worshipping God and proclaiming that at the very heart of the universe lies God's rule, God's splendour and God's majesty. In a world where we are surrounded by enemies and lies, we need to praise God in this manner. It is the pattern not just of this prayer but of the entire Bible. The book of Psalms ends with a great exultant shout: 'Let everything that lives sing praises to the LORD! Praise the LORD!' The book of Revelation, which concludes God's written word, is full of great songs of triumph echoing this theme that the kingdom, the power and the glory are God's for ever.

In praying these words we are also defying all the powers that are opposed to God. Can you imagine how the devil hates this phrase – *all* the kingdom and *all* the power and *all* the glory belong to God and to God *alone?* There is nothing left for anybody else. By saying this little phrase we go against all other powers, structures and organisations that seek to rule this world. When we say it, we challenge all media giants, all armies, all governments, all multinational corporations and all empires of technology. In these words, we tell them all that to God and God alone belongs all praise, majesty and rule because his alone is the kingdom, the power and the glory. These words could easily be the most subversive statement ever written!

In praying these words we want to proclaim this truth, not just in our lives, in our homes or in our churches, but also in the world. We want to tell out across the entire world the good news of how the kingdom and the power and the glory of God can be known in Jesus Christ.

Finally, in praying these words we are proclaiming to all creation the joyful certainty of God's ultimate victory. We have been shown the future and it belongs to God. The victory of Jesus is certain. Anything that does not belong to him is temporary and will soon pass away. One day, to say of God, 'Yours is the kingdom, the power and the glory' will not be a statement of faith; it will be the triumphant acknowledgement of a completed and eternal fact.

And until that great day dawns may we allow this prayer to shape our worship and our lives to the eternal glory of God – Father, Son and Holy Spirit – to whom belongs the kingdom, the power and the glory for ever. *Amen.*

# Further Reading

The following is a list of resources for further study. In some cases, particularly the commentaries, the Lord's Prayer is covered in only a part of the book.

Carson, D. A., 'Matthew' in F. E. Gaebelein (ed.), *The Expositor's Bible Commentary*, Vol. 8. Zondervan, 1984, pp. 3–599.

Dunn, J. D. G., 'Prayer' in J. B. Green and S. McKnight (eds), *The Dictionary of Jesus and the Gospels*. InterVarsity Press, 1992, pp. 617–624.

Forster, R. J., *Prayer: Finding the Heart's True Home*. HarperCollins, 1992, p. 256.

France, R. T., 'Matthew' in *Tyndale New Testament Commentaries*. InterVarsity Press, 1985.

Hagner, D. A., 'Matthew 1–13' in *Word Biblical Commentary*, 33a. Word, 1993.

Keener, C. S., 'Matthew' in *IVP New Testament Commentary*, Series 1. InterVarsity Press, 1997.

Mounce, R. H., 'Matthew' in *New International Biblical Commentary*. Hendrickson & Paternoster Press, 1991.

Stibbe, Mark, *From Orphans to Heirs*. Bible Reading Fellowship, 1999.

Stott, J. R. W., *The Message of the Sermon on the Mount*, The Bible Speaks Today. InterVarsity Press, 1978, 1988.

Woolmer, John, *Thinking Clearly about Prayer*. Monarch, 1997.

Wright, Tom, *The Lord and His Prayer*. Triangle, 1996.

# Contact Details

If you would like to know more about the ministry of J. John, or order books and resources, please contact:

The Philo Trust
141 High Street
Rickmansworth
WD3 1AR
admin@philotrust.com

or visit the website at www.philotrust.com

The Philo Trust is the charity which supports the ministry of J. John. The word Philo is Greek for brotherly love.

The Philo Trust was launched as a registered charity in 1980. Since then it has enabled J. John to lead nearly 200 missions throughout the UK and overseas, developing many innovative approaches to communicating the message of Christianity.

J. John is also a prolific writer, currently having 14 titles in print in 13 languages.

# Ten

**Living the Ten Commandments in the Twenty-first Century**

## by J. John

Imagine a world where people loved each other. What would it look like? How would people behave towards one another?

J. John explores an ancient code of behaviour that provides a window on life as it should be – life as it could be – where respect for others and for God determines everything we do.

The name that code normally goes by is the Ten Commandments. But be prepared for a few surprises.

*'You will not be able to put it down . . .'*
> – ANDY REED
> MP for Loughborough

*'Christian teaching at its very best . . .'*
> – RABBI DR JEREMY ROSEN

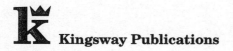 **Kingsway Publications**